How to be your own (best) Tennis Pro

Paul Johan Stokstad

This book is dedicated to "Coach" Lloyd Stokstad, who is still a student of the game, and a master pro for the rest of us.

•Austin •Fairfield •Delhi

How to be your own (best)Tennis Pro
Paul Johan Stokstad

© 1st World Library – Literary Society, 2003
809 South 2nd Street
Fairfield, IA 52556
www.1stworldlibrary.org
First Edition

LCCN: 2003110591

ISBN: 1887472983

All rights reserved. No part of this book may be reproduced or utilized in any form or by any means, electronic or mechanical, including photocopying or recording, or by any information storage and retrieval system, without permission in writing from the publisher.

Readers interested in obtaining information on 1stWorld Library: •Publishing Services •Contributions •Book Conversion • Convert-On-Demand / Print-On-Demand contact www.1stworldlibrary.org

Contents

How to use this book 5

Preface 7

Introduction 11

Chapter 1
Becoming Your Own Tennis Pro 15

Chapter 2
Introduction to Point Projects: takin' it to the streets 25

Chapter 3
Point Projects in Practice: Doing What the Man said 33

Chapter 4
Point Projects and Competitive Matches: Or, how to use everybody else to get better Yourself 47

Chapter 5
Point Projects in the Gap Between the Strokes 53

Chapter 6
Point Projects for the Forehand.................. 67

Chapter 7
Point Projects for the Backhand.................. 81

Chapter 8
Point Projects for the Serve.........................89

Chapter 9
Point Projects for the Serve Return...............99

Chapter 10
Point Projects for the Overhead..................105

Chapter 11
Point Projects for the Volley...................... 109

Chapter 12
Now What?...115

Appendix A.. 117

Appendix B... 119

Appendix C..125

About the Author....................................127

How to use this book

This book is not designed to teach you how to play tennis. It's intended to show you how to practice and improve your game effectively. It does not replace professional instruction. I would assume that it is self-evident that it would be harder to become a tennis pro than it would be to become a tennis player. This book takes you down the road that a professional takes when he/she looks at your game, and gives you some tools to analyze and integrate new tennis skills into your game. You will only have one student to worry about: yourself. The book presents an innovative way of practicing tennis skills, a method that you can use to take notes on lessons and matches and come up with personal projects for subsequent practice. I do provide a number of sample tennis tips of use for both beginners and more advanced players. But the point is learn to pick and choose your own projects as you begin to take a professional's attitude and approach toward your own game.

I begin chapter five and subsequent chapters with a discussion of the typical things that pros tell beginning players and then go on to describe some of the points that I look for in my own students and in my own game. Hopefully that will help you start to develop your own lists of points for incorporation into your tennis game.

Preface

Don't give up your day pro.

As I have indicated, despite the title of this book, it's not intended to wean you off of formal tennis instruction, nor is it enough to just read it and start playing. You need lessons, from a qualified profess- ional (see appendix C). This book is about helping you to take responsibility for your own tennis development, applying the attitudes and techniques of a professional to your own learning process. You will also learn how to more effectively apply on court what you learn about tennis from all sources, including friends, tennis magazines and books, tennis on television, your own experience, and professional instruction.

Another thing to know is that I can't be your tennis pro, either. I wish I could meet each and every one of you and talk about your game. But I can't because there is only one me and I hope that there will be a lot of you. But that's where the other tennis teachers come in. And that's why we have a big society, because we need plenty of people to help all of the other people with all of their needs.

I think of the other pros as my professional buddies, my representatives. They can work with you because I can't teach everyone. The trained pro standing with you is far more important than the greatest tennis pro in the world who is two thousand (or even two) miles away. You can learn something from a book, and from a distance, but not everything. A trained eye looking at what you are doing is extremely valuable.

The fact is that I don't want to replace your pro, I want him or her to have full authority to present ideas to you as your original authority on the sport. I have included many chapters in this book describing techniques of how to hit various tennis shots. But I would be perfectly happy if you followed none of my advice on how to hit the ball. You could skip those chapters entirely and still get the main message of this book, which is to develop your own list of projects that you are going to apply to every aspect of your game, based on what you have heard, read or seen.

When you do that, you start to become your own best tennis pro. When you take a professional attitude toward your own tennis development, you will extend what you learn from lessons and books and apply it more effectively, becoming a co-creator of your own tennis game. I can assure you that finding a student who takes tennis as seriously as that will be a wonderful experience for your pro, and they will happily move into the role of a facilitator, collaborating with you as you grow your own game.

On the other hand, I have included some insights into every major tennis stroke and even the time gap between the strokes, based on forty years of playing, teaching, and studying the game. That's what makes me my own best tennis pro. But then I had great teachers, all the way from Pancho Gonzales, Jack Kramer, Lew Hoad, Rod Laver, Pancho Segura and Tony Trabert on down through Borg, McEnroe, Lendl, Courier, Agassi, Sampras, Vic Braden and, just today, Lleyton Hewitt. I've learned great tennis from everybody, but of course, mostly from my father, Lloyd Stokstad, who spent time in the forties and fifties watching the early guys play, formulated his own systems, and became Iowa's first full-time teaching pro.

And you can gather all that knowledge and more, plus making it a real part of your game, using the material and the methods in this book.

For my part, I've always had to be my own best pro, because by the time tennis got my full attention my father was teaching paying clients and I was the ball retriever. So, you could say, I've never really had a single lesson. But I watched, and listened, and helped teach, and absorbed, and although I probably would have gone farther in the competitive world if I had been able to hang out at a fulltime tennis academy from age 6, I've still come a long way, and it's not over yet. It's a constant process of growth, as far as I'm concerned. And that's how it should be.

Introduction

Static versus Process Players

You might play tennis like this: you have some buddies, you all play about on the same level, you get together once or twice a week, hit on court for about ten minutes and then start playing doubles. Maybe you are like that. That's a fine activity. It's good exercise and it's fun. But, if you plan to stay that way, this book is not for you.

A player like that is a static player. Not really improving. They are just riding on whatever tennis skill level that they achieved through an initial battery of lessons, clinics, and maybe a year or two of high school or junior tennis, and now they are cruising. Depending on how rested they are, or whether their serve is on or off, they have a good or bad day on the court. If you want to stay like that, this book is not for you, unless you are going to buy it and give it as a gift to a *process player*.

A process player looks at his or her tennis game as a

constant process of growth and expansion to a new level of excellence. To grow as a tennis player you need to do more than play once or twice a week with a ten-minute warm-up. Or, if you do only have that much time to play, you have to approach your tennis play with an "it's a work in progress" attitude, and use the time that you do have to try out and stabilize new skills.

A process player is focused on the process of growth and may even take delight in stabilizing the tiniest aspect of their game as a contribution to the overall process of developing a bigger game. They may not be constantly focused on winning, but rather give attention to the elements that, when put together, tend to create more wins. This type of player places both winning and losing into a larger context of an overall process of growth in tennis skills, knowledge, and achievement.

Such a player is on a permanent quest for improvement. When you step off of the train of improvement, you're stuck in a little backwater town with little chance of growth. A complete, growing tennis player is like a three-legged stool, where one leg is instruction, the second is practice, and the third is play. If you have all three of these elements in your tennis experience you are probably having a fairly complete experience of tennis as a growth process.

Most beginning players are big on instruction, practice a little, and play when they can, if they can get the ball in the court at all. Advanced beginners continue instruction, may practice now and then, and have started to play together. More advanced (club level) players have generally abandoned lessons and practice and simply play, play, play.

Only the middle group has a complete experience. Once you step out of the middle category into the last group, your growth is at a standstill, and, in a way, your tennis starts to die. It starts to die because you can't really improve much, and your success is only determined by your physical fitness, age, or other non-tennis skill related factors.

If you aren't constantly growing, you are slowly dying. At least that's the way I look at it.

Imagine doing a play with no rehearsal. Sure you studied drama in college, but you're going to get up there in front of everybody and just wing it. Not that you couldn't wing it to some degree, but you're going to have a much more comfortable experience if you've rehearsed a bit. If you have hit 200 practice serves this week, when you get on court in your weekly doubles match you are not going to spend time in the warm-up trying to remember your serve (like mentally reviewing your lines when you are already onstage), you're going to show what you've stabilized in practice/rehearsal.

Of course, there is a type of theatre where you get onstage and perform without any memorization: improvisational theatre (don't get me started - I love improv!). In improv theatre you get up and create things on the spot. And improv, since it's based on playing theatre games together, is quite analogous to a tennis game, where you have to make up a new interaction on every point. But what you may not know is that improv theatre performers rehearse for hours in order to understand and perfect techniques of group agreement, vivid physicality, mime, dance, singing, and group trust in order to prepare for their apparently spontaneous outbursts of creativity. They are being spontaneous. But within a carefully structured system of rules and developed competencies that tend to support success in their game playing.

Like that, a tennis player needs to practice tennis outside of matches in order to bring something new to the table. A match reveals your strengths and weaknesses. Practice and instruction fixes weaknesses and enhances strengths so that you can get back on the court on a higher level of accomplishment.

This book offers a technique of practice that ensures that the things that you learn from your pro, from watching professionals play and from reading about tennis find their way out on the court to enrich your game tremendously. But none of this will work unless you have a growth process approach to tennis. Great tennis is played by people who are curious about how great they can be, relentlessly pursue excellence, and use every tennis moment to maximize their skill development.

Not that you can't PLAY tennis. Just play with a purpose. This book shows you how.

Chapter 1.

Becoming Your Own Tennis Pro

Let's think a moment about what it would take to become a tennis professional. A teaching pro, that is. Probably you would start with years of tennis play. Probably you would have received excellent instruction of some kind, taking lessons from established pros here and there. From participating in their drills and watching their instructional methods, you may acquire some building blocks of how a lesson might be structured, of various drills that could be used to teach tennis skills, and a number of phrases that stick in your head about how to hit the ball.

Based on all that you may read about tennis, watch tennis on television, and try to learn from what you see the playing pros do. Then you may actually take instruction of some kind in teaching tennis, attending a professional tennis teaching school. Or you may apprentice yourself to an established pro, helping them with lessons and clinics. Finally, you may hear of a full-time position somewhere and get hired.

In short, you become a pro. As a professional you may continue your development by becoming certified by one of the tennis professional associations (USPTA or USPTR, in the U.S.). Through those organizations you may take ongoing training in sports science, motivational training, tactics, etc., in order to have more to offer your students.

That's a believable route to the goal of becoming a teaching tennis professional. But that's not what this book is about. It's about helping you become your own tennis professional, or at least the best one in the world for you.

How can I say that you will be your own best pro? First of all, unless you are phenomenally wealthy, you don't have the money to take all of the instruction you might want. Second of all, if you begin taking a hand in your own development as a tennis player, you have several advantages over all of the other pros in the world: (1) you are always there when you need you, (2) you can coach yourself on court all the time, before during and after every point, game, set or match, and (3) you only have one student to worry about.

What you are really doing when you become your own best tennis pro is taking the attitude toward your game that a pro would have. A pro looks at your game as a developing process. A pro studies the game of tennis, plus studying your game, and tries to come up with ways to take you to the next skill level.

If you acquire that attitude, that tennis is a curiosity, a fascinating interplay of biomechanics, physics, timing, conditioning, mathematics, psychology, lighting conditions, nutrition, aerobics, and equipment, and that all of those areas deserve attention, you're on your way to becoming your own (best) pro.

What You Can Do to Start:

First of all, you can begin deserving the complement that my father, who has been teaching championship players for over fifty years, gives to his prize students, when he calls them a "student of the game." That means that you will start observing the game of tennis and try to see what makes it work. You will watch professional players and see how they hit a forehand. You will watch what you are doing when you hit the ball.

Every time a professional player hits a shot he or she is, in a sense, making a loud statement to anyone who can hear: "This is a forehand!" or "This is how you hit the serve, dude." All of their weapons are visible to those who know what to look for. To a teaching pro, watching the playing pros is a feast of information.

Not to say that all of the "statements" by the playing pros are the same. Not at all. But each one takes a position, of a sort. "I'm Marcelo Rios, and I hit a powerful, high, looping, deep ball, holding the racket with my first knuckle on the bottom of the racket." Or, "I'm Gustavo Kuerten and sometimes on my backhand on the backswing, in addition to my shoulder turn I also let my elbow bend a little, which gives me some extra racket head speed when I straighten my elbow out on the way up through the ball."

Even though they each speak a different tennis language, they are all clearly comprehensible to those who are listening on the sidelines, while the players engage in a fascinating tennis debate with their opponent. And therein lies the charm of competition among the great... an ongoing series of statements about what great tennis is... as each great player inspires the other to come up with a more complete statement of total tennis development.

One player asks the question, "Can you hit this?" (An inside out forehand to the backhand corner). The other responds with "of course, but what's your thought about this?" (a down the line under spin shot). And you can listen and learn.

In addition to "listening" to the pros, you can gather information from other sources, from matches that you've played, from tennis books, tennis magazines, and (mainly) by taking lessons from a certified pro.

I know I said that you'd become your own best tennis pro, but not that you'd become your only tennis pro. Even the pros have coaches. It's just that you're the only person who can take that coaching out on the court. So you've got to be the best.

The things that your pro tells you are the main things that you want to apply using the techniques that I will describe in this book. What makes you better than your pro (in addition to what I have already mentioned), is that you are going to take his or her theories and apply them. Your pro can only present the information, and occasionally evaluate the results. Using the techniques in this book, you can make sure that what your pro tells you finds it's way deep into every corner of how you play the game.

You are going to learn to use those phrases that you hear over and over, "bend your knees," "turn your shoulder," "low to high," "eye on the ball," etc. and make those things real parts of your game so that they become automatic in the most trying of game day situations.

Mini-Lessons:

Another source of information is what I call mini-lessons. Every point that you play is a mini-lesson. Something happened. If you won the point, most of the time you executed your strokes and strategy successfully and your opponent made some error. Occasionally you win a point outright, without an obvious technical error by your opponent.

If you lost the point, you have an interesting riddle to decipher: where did I go wrong, what did I do that held me back from success, and what can I do to my preparation, strategy or execution to make sure that trend doesn't continue. Sometimes you learn the most from your mistakes.

Looking at points and even individual strokes as mini-lessons puts your attention on the fine details of the sport. It is this attention to detail that is required to move ahead to the next skill level. Putting attention on both good and bad results will give lots of useful information.

I believe that excellence in anything results from simply paying attention. That's such an interesting concept: your attention, as a form of currency, almost, that you can spend. Think of your attention as a sort of magic flashlight that you can shine onto any subject, and yet, unlike a flashlight, the subject will stay illumined once you have found it.

In observing things we normally move from the general to the specific. You might say, "I hit my forehand." And then, you might move through a series of more detailed analyses:

1. I hit my forehand.

2. I turned my shoulder as the ball came to me and I kept my eye on the ball and I hit my forehand

3. As soon as I realized that it was a forehand I turned my entire body and set my racket and my non-hitting hand back, then I moved to the ball, got my feet set, my knees bent, and turned my torso as the ball came to me and I started my stroke way below the ball and came up through it, keeping my eye on the ball all the way to the racket, and then I continued my stroke, catching the racket with my non-dominant hand as I turned back to prepare for the next shot.

4. As my (previous) ball flew to him I got in position and as he swung I did a split step, and watched the ball the entire time as he hit it and then as the ball rose in the air toward me as I turned my entire body to the forehand side,

offloading from the ground and as if floating up while the ball floated up, moved to the side fully turned and prepared to hit and as the ball fell to bounce on my side I brought my weight down, too, so that I had my feet set as the ball bounced and as it rose again I brought my body around as a unit and powered up through my legs and brought the racket up through the ball, intersecting the line of flight of the ball while watching the seams of the ball spin with a quiet fascination, releasing my wrist upward through the ball in a 45 degree angle as I caught the racket in my non-dominant hand, all the time exhaling freely through the shot while watching the flight of my ball and analyzing the racket preparation of my opponent.

The point is that you can analyze your shot in greater and greater detail. By doing this, you become more and more aware of what you are actually doing. By taking the machine apart and looking at the pieces, we can gain a greater awareness of how it all goes together.

I believe that many people don't actually "have" a forehand (for example). They have an approximation of a forehand, a general behavior that they engage in when the ball lands on their forehand side. But they don't really have a consistent forehand shot that they hit every time, partially because they haven't practiced it enough, and partially due to the fact that they let the rapid and uncontrolled movement of their opponent's ball distort their shots.

And yet, a consistent shot is what we really want. The whole idea is to hit your shot, not some abbreviated improvisation that you came up with because your opponent hit too hard, or you were running, etc. We would like to hit the perfect forehand every time.

If your name was Pete Sampras I would call your forehand "the Sampras forehand." If it was Schmulewitz I would call it the "Schmulewitz forehand." What we are trying to do is stabilize what the Schmulewitz forehand is (perhaps modeling it on the Sampras one) and hit that as many times as possible.

To stabilize what the Schmulewitz forehand actually is, we need to hit a lot of them in practice and then we will have something that we can rely on as a consistent element in matches.

Then we do everything that we can between shots to try to hit a shot that is as similar to the prototypical Schmulewitz forehand as possible: we move to the ball, get set, and hit. By moving to the ball and getting set we are eliminating the variables that keep us from hitting our own forehand.

By analyzing our shot in detail and making focused adjustments to it in practice, we will finally have a stabilized, known entity to use when we are out there in competitive play.

It's an odd thing, but in my teaching experience, the better the player I'm working with, the more some tiny correction will make an enormous difference. The reasons for this are easy to discern, since the beginning player has no consistency. They hit the ball in a new way almost every time they hit. But an established player has developed systems for how to hit the ball. Hopefully they had some instruction so that those systems are effective, but in any case they have a recognizable style of play. If someone has an established habit pattern, then a tiny change will make a big difference.

That's why competitive tennis players (and golfers!) are always experimenting with adjustments to their stroke, stance, etc. They are looking for the breakthrough tweak that will bring their game up to the next level of excellence.

The challenge is that once we have broken the strokes down into all of these pieces, it's impossible to remember everything while we are on court. That's why the beginning player is overwhelmed. It's all intellectual instruction for them, there's no muscle memory. Plus, some experts say that the mind can only effectively focus on one thing at a time.

To combat this, we pay attention to what we are doing, break it down into pieces, and then practice just one piece of the puzzle at a time, before reassembling it all as a complete tennis game.

All of this detailed analysis, gained by watching the pros, reading tennis magazines, learning from your pro and a close personal (and video-taped) inspection of your own play, sets you on the road to becoming your own best tennis pro. The next chapter gives you an engine to speed you on your way.

Chapter 2

Introduction to Point Projects: takin' it to the streets

The concept is simple. You take some aspect of the game, some instruction that you have received, and focus on that particular item while engaged in practice or match play. For example, your tennis pro may have taught you to get your feet set before hitting the ball. Of course, he may also have told you to get your racket back quickly, keep your eyes on the ball, make a shoulder turn, bring your non-dominant hand back with your other hand, change grips properly, do a skip step as the opponent hits, hit the ball out in front, hit from low to high, bend your knees and then straighten them on the hit, follow through high, and a number of other things. But instead of trying to remember all of that, you are simply going to play a tennis point, or rally with someone, with the emphasis on one of those projects, i.e. - getting your feet set before hitting the ball.

With this single "point project" in mind, you simply

make sure that, regardless of whatever else happens, you WILL get your feet set before hitting the ball, if at all possible. You may miss the ball completely, you may hit it over the fence, you may do any number of other things wrong, but at least for this one point you promise yourself that you are going to have your feet set when you hit the ball.

There are several good effects of this practice technique. First of all, you feel successful no matter what happened to your tennis shots. Sure you want to get the ball over the net, sure you want to send it scorching past your opponent, but, regardless of the fact that you muffed the ball into the net, if you accomplished your point project, you have achieved some level of success. You may have lost the point, you may have forgotten for the moment every other point of instruction that you have ever received, but you did (to some degree) achieve your project of getting your feet set.

Having stabilized that, you can move on to the next variable.

It's like building a house from scratch. First you have to make one good brick. Then you have to make another good brick, and then another. And then you have to put in one electrical wire that works, and then hook up a light bulb. Just keep doing one good thing at a time, building on the foundation of the other good things and eventually you have a house (hopefully with a tennis court out back).

What a point project does is give you a handle on the complicated behavior of taking a stick in your hand, running, stopping, turning your body and hitting a little round fuzzy thing back over a net to a planned destination on the other side of the net to a person who hopes you won't be able to do it. You just stabilize one of those behaviors at a time and eventually it all becomes smooth.

The other good thing about point projects is they are generally things that help get your shot over into your opponent's court. In other words, it's not just that you feel good that you achieved your point project of getting your feet set, it's that the by-product of achieving that point-project is the effect that achievement has on your stroke, i.e. - you are far more likely to hit a good forehand with your feet set than if you are hitting it on the dead run.

So, we break the complicated behavior of tennis down into little pieces, get good at the pieces, and then reassemble it all as a total tennis game.

The other big effect of point projects, and the key to becoming your own (best) tennis pro, is the power that this method gives to get things that you learn in lessons out of the abstract and into your real game day play. It's one thing to learn some new skill or principle in a tennis lesson, but it's another thing entirely to remember that point when you are playing or even competing with another person. But that is the best place for applying what you have learned.

Don't get me wrong, I don't think that you should spend every competitive tennis match focusing on whether your feet are set. As a matter of fact, it's much better if it has become an automatic habit, and you don't have to think about it at all. It's just "on the way to automatic" that we want you to use the technique.

When you're competing it's probably better that you just enjoy yourself, let your skills express themselves, and analyze later.

You might ask how this is different from what we are already doing. It's a subtle difference, but subtle things can be powerful. To understand this, we need to look at how lessons are taught, since, in a way, lessons are both good and bad for you. In order to teach the absolute beginner we normally simplify the tasks. Maybe we don't even try to have you hit over that net. We show you how to hold the racket. We introduce you to some strokes. We drop the ball nicely into your hitting zone so that you can practice that stroke. Then we move twenty feet away and carefully toss the ball toward your hitting zone. Then we have you start moving to the ball, getting your feet set and hitting the ball that you have to run for. And we progress from there.

Throughout this instruction you will hear any number of comments from your pro, such as shoulder turn, racket back, low to high hit, eyes on the ball, etc.

What's unusual about all this is the spoon-fed quality that it all has. The pro hits the ball right to you at a perfect pace (or tries to, anyway). That spoon-fed training is good for a beginner, but unless your pro moves you systematically into hitting balls on the run, you are in for a wake-up call when you try to hit with a real human being. Real human beings come in three forms:

    1) Superhuman: Your pro who can feed you nice balls all day.

2) Inhuman: An experienced player, who unless he is married to you, hits the ball too hard and is TRYING to make you miss.

3) Subhuman, another beginner like you, who can't hit the ball back in the same place twice

What this means is that we train one way but play another. The idea of this book is to take the training comments that your pro gives you and apply them in playing situations. So, you will take notes on what she says, and when you are playing, you will stabilize those skills in actual game-play situations. With the point project method, you use warm-ups and practice matches to stabilize aspects of your evolving tennis game.

When you analyze your tennis activities, how many of your matches are intense rivalries that demand perfect concentration and performance? A lot, maybe, if you are on a competitive high school or college team, or play in a league of some sort. But probably a reasonable amount of your tennis time is spent playing matches or hitting with people where the outcome isn't crucial to your survival.

In practice matches, and while warming up or rallying with a friend, you can take the opportunity of using that game-like situation to stabilize your new backswing, or incorporate that new shoulder turn, etc.

This tool, while maybe a distraction during match Play–anything can be overused–can be effectively applied in a number of tennis situations. For example, when you are drilling with a friend, hitting with a ball machine, hitting against a wall, warming up for a match, when you are in a match and feel like you are losing concentration or not playing up to your usual level, or when you are playing someone on a far higher or lower skill level than you. I will discuss these situations in more detail in later chapters.

There's a story about simple point projects like this, true or not, and it involves Arthur Ashe. The story is that he's playing in the Davis Cup where on-court coaching is allowed, and as he switches sides, he consults with the coach. Then he goes out and wins the match. So after the match, the media guy goes up to the coach and asks what significant tactical insight he offered to Arthur to turn the match around. "What?" says the coach, "Oh, that. No big deal. I just told him he needed to hit the ball more out in front." It's not that Arthur Ashe didn't know the value of that. It's just that in the heat of battle, or against this particular opponent, he was slipping a bit in executing that particular variable until the coach pointed it out.

The point is that the changes needed when your game is developed are not sophisticated changes. When your serve is well established and grooved, the tiniest change has an enormous effect. This type of thing, the little change for enormous effect, is the goal of every tennis lesson and every growing tennis player. When your pro can tell you one thing that all of a sudden makes your serve go in, I can assure you it's a great moment for everybody. You're happy because you are all of a sudden experiencing success, the pro is happy because his teaching is working and the sun comes out on the court and smiles down on everybody.

Maybe you have heard the pro say "turn your

shoulder" a hundred times, but when he says "show your back to your opponent before you hit," you finally get it. This is what the pro searches for, the perfect phrase to make the way to greatness clearer to you, the perfect clue that will finally unlock the tennis animal lurking within your game, and set you free to play your best. As players we can sift through these points of instruction, try them out as point projects, until they become automatic behaviors as we pursue the goal of tennis excellence.

If you are struggling on court, the application of one or two of these things will almost always bring your game back to its senses. For me it's keeping my eyes on the ball all the way to contact, turning my shoulder way back, and hitting the ball out in front. Especially on the backhand, I find that early contact on the ball almost always works wonders. You can sift through your point projects as well, and find the ones that are the most valuable, and use them in warm-ups and matches to bring your game to life.

What Next?

To make this book as useful as possible, I have indicated potential point projects in bold face type throughout the book. Anything in this book in bold face type is something that you can apply to your own game, using the point projects method. But the projects that I have emphasized are just a start. Your pro may have many more (and better) points to make about your game. You may have ideas and insights of your own. You may have seen something in a tennis magazine that you want to try out. But regardless of the source or the level of sophistication of the information, the point project scenario is one method of incorporating the new, desired skill into your game.

Chapter 3

Point Projects in Practice
Doing What the Man Said

It's simply that. Do what the Man said. Or, if you have a female pro, it's "if momma ain't happy, ain't nobody happy." Let's face it. You may be your own best tennis pro because you're the cheapest and the most likely to be there when you need one, but maybe you don't yet have quite as much experience and knowledge as one of those REAL pros out there.

Even Pete Sampras got a second opinion. As a matter of fact, Pete Sampras' best game was like having lunch on Rodeo Drive in Beverly Hills: the strawberries are from Mexico, the fish is from Hawaii, the sauce is from France. If what I've heard is correct, Pete got his backhand from one guy, his serve from another, and someone else tuned up his volley. Sure he had an original coach, but he got a lot of second and third opinions to refine his game.

Likewise, even though we want you to realize you can

be your own best tennis coach, it's going to be a while (if ever) before you are the only coach you'll ever need. Pete got help even while he was at the top of the pile. Plus, the one thing you can't do very well is watch yourself play.

You can, however, videotape yourself. I can assure you it's a wakeup call to see yourself play on camera. And if you have gathered any tennis knowledge, it's a serious shock to see what you are actually doing out there. Using a video camera you can see for real what you are doing and then go back to practice and correct (using point projects) what you see.

But a tennis pro can move around better than a camera, and see what you are doing from more angles more effectively. Plus the mind behind the pro's physical vision brings a lot of value-added features to the show.

So, let's say that your pro has told you four or five things in a lesson. It wouldn't hurt to write those things down at the end. Keeping a tennis notebook is one thing that will immediately begin to set you apart from the everyday tennis player. If you start writing things down you start taking responsibility for what's happening to you, your tennis development begins to take on the form of a sort of campaign or plan, and you are starting to think like a tennis pro. That's what we're trying to do here.

Having written those points down, you now have a shopping list of things to practice. Anyone who has ever taken lessons knows that lessons are meaningless without practice in between lessons. I can tell you as a teaching pro that nothing is more empty than giving a lesson once a week to someone who only plays tennis once a week - in my lesson. The student hasn't stabilized anything new, and has only deteriorated since the last lesson. You have to virtually start all over. You feel, as a coach, that the student is doing nothing to help himself. It's no fun. It's money, but not fun money.

But you are a different sort. You are a process player, taking responsibility for your own growth. You are going to have a professional attitude about your own tennis development. Taking those points from your pro out on the court, you are going to practice them, one by one, until you stabilize and own them.

You can practice stroking and court movement skills using a ball machine, a hitting wall, a hitting partner, with pre-visualization, in warm-ups, or in practice matches. Let's look at each of these in detail:

With The Ball Machine

For a beginner, it may be way more important to hit with a ball machine than it is to hit with another beginner. Against the ball machine, you generally don't have to worry about where the ball is going to land. Direction is more or less established. Varying quality of the tennis balls in the machine may cause longer or shorter bounces, but at least the direction of the ball is set.

In that case you can forget about movement to the ball and just focus on point one that you got from your pro. See if you can establish that one skill before moving on to the next item on your list. Sometimes I'll hit ten balls focusing on point project number one, and ten focusing on number two, etc., and then cycle back through the list, if time allows.

As your skill level with the projects that you are developing grows you can add variables such as moving to the ball and hitting it, or setting the ball machine to oscillate the feed from side to side, maintaining the integrity of the original point project behavior along with the added complexity of foot movement.

Against the Wall

Doing point projects against a wall is a lot like doing it against a ball machine, since you have a pretty good idea of where the ball is going to land. But there are subtle differences. First of all, a hitting wall is a secret childhood (and grownup) friend of many a great player. Supposedly John McEnroe said, "Forget the tennis camps, just hit against the wall." Regardless of whether he really said that or not, the sentiment has an element of truth. Tennis camps can be a great help to your game. But nothing replaces basic practice. It's the tennis version of "How do you get to Carnegie Hall" (now say "practice" out loud three times).

There are little tricks to make wall practice more game-like, and therefore more useful. One great thing to do, though you rarely have control over this variable, is to hit against a big wall. The little eight feet high, eight feet wide walls that you find at public courts don't do tennis practice justice. Fifteen or twenty feet high for the width of a tennis court is more like it. In the latter case you can hit higher balls, hit with a greater margin for error (important for beginners.... who are, in most cases, the ones using the wall).

The little walls with the white line 3 feet above the court train players to hit low balls. The fact is that hitting low hard balls is only one of the many possibilities in tennis. Most pros ask you to use height to create depth. Vic Braden describes tennis as a "lifting game." That means we want to hit the ball six or eight feet over the net in order to have it land properly in the back court. To train for that, it's great to have a hitting wall that is at least that high or higher.

Training with a wall involves some creativity if you want to simulate game-like conditions. First of all, even if you stand back from the wall the same distance as you would stand from the net on court, the ball will probably come back too fast. That's because when you rally with someone on a real court the ball usually travels twice as far. That means that the ball hit against the wall is too fast to be game-like.

For a beginner this is devastating to all of his or her good intentions to hit the ball the way the pro told him. One half second after the beginner has tossed up the ball, waited for it to bounce, and then hit a mighty, fairly well formed forehand, the ball is back demanding another perfect forehand. The student scrambles to hit it, and makes up a new shot, unrehearsed, not resembling the shot he was trained to do at all.

This is one difference between the beginner and the established player. The beginner has many more stroke varieties than the experienced player.

Someone once asked a comedian the secret of his success, and he replied, "Get yourself a killer routine, and keep changing the audience." It's the same thing in tennis. Get yourself a great forehand, and keep changing the location that you hit it from. The established player has eliminated the variables from her stroke, as much as possible, and simply moves her feet around to set up and hit that same stroke effectively.

So, when hitting against the wall, we do several things to give ourselves more time to hit the perfect stroke that we are trying to stabilize. One thing you can do is to **hit that stroke once, and then catch** the returning ball. What this does is allow you to hit a number of balls, putting your attention on the perfection of your technique, while not worrying about hitting another one right away.

Another "against the wall" technique is to **let the ball bounce two or three times** before hitting it. Usually two times is enough. This goes against the rigorous on-court demand that you not practice letting the ball bounce twice. It's a good rule when you are rallying with someone else, because what you do in practice tends to be what you do in matches.

But against the wall you can break that rule, because you want to give yourself more time to take your real wind-up and hit your full stroke. You can use this effect on the volley, too, and let the ball bounce once to simulate the amount of time that you would normally have on your volley.

Then you can turn this idea around and use the wall conventionally, realizing that the ball is coming back too fast, and turn that to your advantage, by practicing your serve return and/or your counter-punching shot (use less backswing), letting the ball bounce only once.

Similarly, when you practice your volley with no bounces, you are practicing at a shot-exchange speed far above what you should need in a match, which prepares you for quick movement in match play.

With a Camcorder

If you have a video camcorder, you have a great opportunity to see if you are really doing what you think you are doing. One difference between the guy you are paying (the pro) and yourself is simply the fact that he can see your every move and you can't. You may think that you are bending your knees and exploding up into the serve, but the camera will probably tell you that it is a less than dramatic knee bend that you are getting. You may think that you are getting a good shoulder turn in before you hit the ball, but Mr. Camcorder may tattle that you are usually only standing with your shoulders at a right angle to the net and using the strength of your arm to hit the ball.

Of course, having a camcorder is only of use if you know what to look for. On the other hand, anyone who has had a single tennis lesson has typically been bombarded by instructional statements. The camera can tell you whether you are actually following those instructions or not.

Here are some ways to use video to self-train:

1. Set the camera on the side of the court, and have a friend or (even better) a ball machine feed balls to you. What you are looking for with a side view is point of contact with the ball, among other things, The point of contact with most ground strokes is in front of the body. If the ball gets in to the body I always say that the ball is playing you rather than that you are playing the ball. We are of course also looking at many other elements we hope to stabilize, such as watching the ball all the way to the racket, feet set on the hit (before, if possible), shoulder turn, etc. We would also typically like to see the racket penetrating the line of flight of the ball from low to high, at least on a topspin shot. On a serve we can evaluate our toss in terms of how high it is and how far forward we've tossed it into the court

2. Set the camera behind you, and again have the ball machine feed you. In this position we can decipher the degree to which we are getting a good shoulder turn before the hit. This is true of both the serve and a groundstroke. We can also use this position to evaluate underspin and volleyed shots, which typically do not include a follow through to the other side of the body (more on this later). This position is also excellent for noting whether you have a "chicken wing" configuration on your forehand, which would be a stroke pattern where your arm goes farther back than your shoulder on the backswing. We don't typically want the

arm to get behind the imaginary line extending out of the shoulder on the backswing. This is a typical behavior of someone who is "arming the ball" rather than engaging the power of the torso by turning their back away from the shot in the preparatory phase and then uncoiling into the hit.

3. Pulling the camera back to the side you can then videotape actual points or an entire set from that perspective in actual play situations. This will enable you to analyze factors such as foot preparedness, i.e. - did you have your feet set on the shot, or were you typically running while you hit. You can also analyze your tactical awareness, shot selection, etc. It may also be valuable to have the camera on that side when your opponent is playing there in order to gauge the depth of your shots to him/her. Then you can reposition the camera again, in the back of the court on your side, to get that perspective on your match play.

4. Another thing that you can do is take your camera to your lessons and videotape the pro (for example) hitting forehands on the ad side of the court while you hit forehands on the deuce side. This shows you both what you are doing and what you should be doing at the same time. If you have a ball machine that oscillates, you can have the ball alternately be fed to the pro and to you and then see what each does with the ball. The non-hitting player can also shadow box a shot while the other is hitting so that you can see the pro's motion and yours side by side and make

subsequent adjustments.

The best kind of camcorder to use is the kind that lets you play back what you just taped on the spot so that you can immediately work on making the changes that you want to make based on the video feedback. But even viewing the awful truth at home is valuable as an inspiration to get out there again and do it right.

Hitting practice

If you are really lucky, you have a drill partner. This is someone who also wants to practice and get better at the game, but doesn't necessarily need to beat you every time you meet in order to feel like she's had a good week. With this person you can work on things that you are trying to stabilize, feed each other balls to help establish new strokes, play mini-matches, hit cross court rallies, etc., just to stabilize your skills without the pressure of competition. This person is worth their weight in tennis coaches, and the price is right.

While warming up with your (lucky you!) drill partner you can again use the ten-ball drill. Hit ten balls focusing on each of the basics, and add in some new point project at the end. This is like doing a pre-flight check before flying a plane. It may not always be necessary, but something tells me that if you are up in the air and your engine dies, a spark plug blows, your flaps don't work or your hydraulic system is drained, your life is all of a sudden a question mark.

Similarly, when you get on court, the first thing to do

is to check that your eyes are following the ball, that you are turning your shoulder right away, that you are hitting the ball out in front, getting your feet set, etc. By doing that, let's say by hitting ten balls focusing on each of those variables, you shake out the cobwebs, remind yourself that you are no longer at the office, get your mind and body tuned up for the task at hand–tennis–and get into the game with your game wide awake. That's good.

Having done that, you can add in one of the points that your pro has mentioned, or that you picked up from Tennis magazine, or wherever you got it. Usually these points are something simple. I consider my serve to be a fairly complicated behavior, but I don't usually work on the whole thing. I work on bending my knees before the shot. I work on tossing the ball farther to the side. I let everything else rest and focus on one aspect of the serve. And then I move on to the next aspect.

Having warmed up effectively, you and your partner may work on some specific stroke or other, or play a few practice games. This is a great time to try to stabilize some new aspect of your game. It's perfect because you are not really competing, and so putting your primary attention on something other than winning is a lot easier.

What you can do in this situation is play real points, but put your attention on something completely different than the outcome of the point. You put your attention on your point project. You focus, for example, on getting your feet set for every ball you hit. You don't even allow yourself to hit unless you can get your feet set. This stabilizes one aspect of proper tennis technique. Having done that, you stabilize something else. That allows you to practice things that you are trying to perfect in actual game conditions. That is the essential point of this book, and valuable practice.

Practice Matches

If you approach practice matches with a developmental attitude, they can be very useful. I consider any match that is not in a tournament or part of league play a practice match. For some people their only competition is playing other local players. In that case you need to find a drill partner. But in any case, you need to have matches where the outcome is not a matter of life and death to your ego.

In a practice match you can again stabilize new skills. Trying out one or maybe two new things is plenty for any match. You've had the instruction. You've been practicing that new forehand; you've drilled with it against the wall, the ball machine, and with your hitting partner. Now it's time to see how that shiny new weapon does in the heat of battle. Even if it's just a minor skirmish.

This is where pre-visualization comes in. When I am going to play a practice match, I think of which aspects of my game I am trying to stabilize. I may even write them down as brief notes to look at between games. Usually it's simple stuff, one to three words. Shoulder turn. Out in front. Split step. Whatever I want to do that day I think about on my way over to the court. I give myself an assignment before I even start to hit.

Plus, I imagine myself doing the behavior properly. **I see myself hitting the ball just the way I want to.** I've heard that the most powerful pre-visualization is to imagine the behavior as if you were actually doing it. That is, it's more powerful to imagine hitting the ball out in front as if you were watching a movie shot out of your own eyes as the hitter than it is to imagine it as if you were watching yourself from a spectator's point of view.

When I step on the court with this mental preparation, I am usually way ahead of my opponent. They just got on court, while I've been there (mentally) for a while. Plus, my practice match with them takes on another quality. Win or lose, it now fits in to an overall process of tennis development that I have going.

I'm using them, in a way, to stabilize a higher level of skill. I may lose the match, but win the war. If I don't mind that my new fledgling serve is not yet as good as my old serve, but have confidence that it is going to be the serve that takes me to the next level of tennis, I go ahead and use it in the match, because it takes me into the future, rather than stabilizing the substandard habits of the past.

In the middle of the match I check in on my agenda now and then. Have I forgotten what I came here for? Am I getting my point projects into play? Or have I drifted into simple competition. In either case, I get on track, and keep up the process-based attitude that will take me to the next skill level.

Chapter 4.

Point Projects and Competitive Matches: Or, how to use everybody else to get better yourself

Consider the following tennis competition scenario involving "the Kid" and "the Coach."

Action: the kid misses a forehand

Kid: "Darn."

Coach, "You suck, I can't believe you missed that easy forehand. You complete dog. Why are you even here?

Action: the kid wins the next point

Coach: "Well, I guess you didn't blow that one at least."

Action: the kid double-faults

Coach: "Throw the ball to the side! To the side, to the

side! How many times do I have to tell you, you complete slime ball?"

If you were watching this little drama in real life, you would probably want to kill the coach.

Why? Because we don't expect coaches to act that way. We expect coaches to be patient, kind, and understanding adults with a mature approach to the overall growth of the student. We expect coaches to come up with solutions to a student's developmental and shot execution problems, and present them in a patient, articulate and balanced manner. We want coaches to motivate but not berate their players. If you are a coach with the modus operandi dramatized above, you will not have students for long.

On the other hand, you can hear a dialogue like this almost any day at a junior tennis tournament when a kid berates himself for missing shots. Sometimes you hear the dialogue out loud. Sometimes it's muttered, or maybe it's just an inner dialogue. Either way, the kid that talks to himself this way isn't yet his own best tennis pro.

You might ask yourself, "What kind of on-court pro am I?" What attitude do I have toward my errors, my successes, and my overall growth on court? When you are playing a real match, take a pro's point of view. If you miss a shot, learn from it. Don't just get mad. If you missed a ball there was a reason for missing it. In some way your system of hitting broke down. This approach to mistakes creates a lot more positive attitude, a kind of curious self-inquiry.

In coaching yourself this way, you may think, "That's

interesting, I missed a shot. I wonder why that is?" Then you come up with a theory: "I did everything right, I turned my body, I got in position, I watched the ball, but still I hit that forehand wider to the right than I wanted to and it went out. I think that their ball must have had more pace on it than usual, and so my usual speed of racket preparation was too long. That means that I have to prepare earlier with this guy so that I never get surprised like that again."

You can turn errors into opportunities. Instead of allowing errors to reflect on your worth as a human being, you treat them as opportunities to perfect yourself. When a tennis pro watches your game, he or she has to evaluate your errors and come up with solutions to make it easy for you to correct them, which should allow you to have more success on court. Now you can begin to do the same thing for yourself.

What this means is that you can always be a winner on court, because you are always learning. You can lose to a more established player and still win in a way, because you used the opportunity to stabilize your game at a higher level. Pete Sampras, when he was twelve, would lose to almost any college level player. But he couldn't let that stop him. Hitting with a college level player would still have been good for young Pete. He would learn that tennis can happen at a higher level of excellence and he would have been challenged to rise to that level.

Similarly, you can learn from playing "worse" players. First of all, the "worse" player is a big challenge. The player who has less pure tennis strokes, who dresses funny, or who doesn't hit the ball as hard as you do, can still have weapons like consistency, variety, disguise, tenacity, and a good attitude. Nothing is more dangerous to the big hitting player than a consistent, unconventional opponent. You're thinking, "I should beat this guy." If you should beat them, then you have nothing to gain. You only have something to lose.

There's always something to gain. The challenge is to play your game, to keep the quality of your tennis up even when the competition level apparently goes down. In that case, you continue focusing on your own game, staying sharp on the details. You can't let the laxness or the softness of your opponent's shots lull you into a sloppiness that takes you out of your strengths. All of a sudden you are playing their game, which they know very well how to win.

You should focus on pulling away. This was supposedly a John McEnroe specialty. He didn't just want to beat you. He wanted to destroy you. If he got ahead, he wanted to get farther ahead. Similarly, I think that, if you can, you should win all the games. You can feel good if you win your serve, or get a "service break." But why not consider that you deserve to win all the games? Not just all your serves and one or two of theirs.

It may sound harsh, but when you play someone in a tournament who really is on a lower level of tennis development than you are, the best thing that you can do for them may be to completely and utterly "McEnroe" (destroy) them. The reason for that is that they are in competition to get better. If you don't give them your best stuff, you don't inspire them to get better. This is especially true when you are only slightly better than your opponent. If they beat you, they aren't inspired to get better. If you beat them, they realize that they still have a way to go to be really good, and should get inspired to do it. I say McEnroll over them. They'll appreciate the lesson in the long run.

If you have the attitude of a coach, you look at competition as a chance to stabilize what you have learned in the heat of battle. You look at your opponent as a co-creator of your best tennis. He or she is there to challenge you to do better. Again, it's sort of a conversation. Your opponent makes a statement about tennis excellence by hitting a forehand crosscourt, you suggest something by hitting down the line, he asks a question by hitting a short cross court ball, you respond with a remark in the form of a drop shot, he runs up and says something over your head with a lob to the backhand corner, you get back into the discussion with an under spin backhand down the line, and so on.

If you are playing with McEnroe, you are having an eloquent discussion about excellent tennis (or more of a lecture, for most people). It was very fascinating watching McEnroe and Borg discuss theories of tennis excellence in the form of tennis balls exchanged over a net a few years ago. And McEnroe seemed to miss the philosophical exchange when it ended with Borg's retirement.

We need our opponents. We both agree to play by certain rules. We both love tennis enough to run around a court in shorts for hours with no pay (usually) hitting a yellow fuzzy thing with a webbed stick. A good boxing coach brings his charge along slowly, exposing him to better and better opponents, leading him to greatness. You can do the same thing with your own game, using your opponents as part of your overall coaching/development plan.

Chapter 5

Point Projects in the Gap Between the Strokes

Beginner Projects:

Eye on the ball: Your pro will almost certainly use this phrase or one of its relatives, such as watch the ball, focus on the ball, etc. It may seem obvious, but, surprisingly, this simple task is often one of the most neglected. I conjecture that this is because the mind is always moving faster than the ball, since it often seems to get ahead of things.

Here are a few ways that players blow this simple instruction in actual practice:

○ They don't start watching the ball until it's too late: On the serve return, for example, some people may not actually pick up where the ball is going until it has almost cleared the net. That is too late. On the serve, you want to start watching the ball before it is hit (more on this later).

- They "check in" on the ball, rather than watch it all the way: It seems that people somehow lose interest in the ball once they have a general idea where it is going. That may be because there are so many other things on their mind, i.e. - running to one side, getting their racket back, getting their feet set, and deciding where on the other guy's side they want to hit the ball.

- They quit watching the ball for the last few feet before the hit: For some reason people seem to lose track of the ball just before the hit.

- They take their eyes off of the ball and put them on the target: Since the mind knows where it wants the ball to go, it naturally jumps ahead to the imagined result.

There are many cures to these problems. One cure is to take the focus of the mind to an even finer degree of detail than the simple "watch the ball" admonition. Some pros will tell you to watch the spin of the seams of the ball. This activity, even more tightly targeted than just tracking the ball through the air, requires an intense focus that can achieve the degree of attention that you really need to hit the ball with certainty.

Another cure is to start watching the ball and never take your eyes off the ball while it is in motion. That means that if you missed the ball your eyes would follow it back to the back fence until it rolled to a stop. Then you can start hitting another ball.

What we are training ourselves to do is to give our visual attention to the ball as tightly as possible. It is amazing what kind of an effect this has on your success in hitting the ball effectively. Even an established player will often find that her strokes acquire 10-20% more certainty and solidity just by watching the ball with intensity.

And I can assure you that the pros are giving it their full attention, since to them it is more than a ball, it's a yellow fuzzy lunch ticket.

Get your feet set:

Your pro has probably said this to you many times, but maybe he hasn't told you why. Maybe he has. The main reason that this one keeps hitting your eardrums is that your pro is trying to simplify matters for you. It's true that a tennis pro can hit the on the dead run at Flushing Meadows while a jet plane is roaring overhead, twenty thousand live spectators are watching, John McEnroe is in the broadcast booth and some girl in the third row is adjusting her halter top. But those are pros. And besides, the pro would much rather eliminate one variable from that scenario, and it's not the jet plane, it's the dead run. The pro doesn't hit on the run because he wants to, it's because he has been forced to do it. He'd much rather get his feet set and whale away with his big forehand.

Unfortunately you don't typically learn to hit the ball while running. The pro feeds you nice underhand tosses, hoping to get your forehand and backhand stabilized. Then you have to learn to move and hit that shot when the ball isn't nicely spoon-fed to you. But even when we move, we want to see if we can get there in time to hit the ball with our feet set, because that's the shot that we learned, not a shot on the run. There is a place for hitting the shot on the run, but it's not your place, just yet, and even the pros don't typically choose to hit that shot.

One thing you need to understand is that if you are going to get your feet set, it has to happen before the shot. That may seem obvious, but it's good to emphasize it. And another thing to understand is that we'd like this "feet set" thing to happen way before the shot, if possible. Some people always get into position just as they hit the ball.

If you plan to arrive at the last minute all of the time, you will sometimes be late. A lazy player will slowly move over and hit the ball at the pace dictated by the incoming ball. A sharp player will move quickly to the ball, get set, and use that extra time to prepare more fully for their shot. If we move quickly, we can stroke at leisure, hitting our best shot rather than some improvisation forced on us by the speed of the ball and our still moving feet.

My "In The Gap" Projects

Some pros are becoming aware that the usual tennis lesson can train you to do something that never happens again. You train getting the ball fed to you exactly where you want it and when you want it. The pro or the ball machine hits the ball to your forehand and you hit your best forehand.

You work hard on grooving your forehand, and eventually get it timed perfectly, but then you go out to play against somebody and only one out of a hundred shots that are hit to you have any resemblance to the shot you have been trained to hit, that is, an underhand toss or a soft forehand right to your hitting zone.

The fact is that you have to be a highly skilled player to hit forehands to a student in the same place every time. It's rare that a student goes out and plays tennis against someone with the skill level of a tennis pro or the consistency of a ball machine. So it's not only that the people that you compete with don't hit the ball where you are used to getting it, they couldn't do it if they tried. Indeed, it's often very challenging to play against a beginner, because nothing that they do is predictable. This is the source of a lot of beginner's luck.

Of course, if your opponent has acquired the skill to direct the ball around the court more or less at will, he will usually hit it somewhere that adds complexity to your problem of returning the ball. They ain't gonna make it easy for ya. Still, using proper stroke preparation, on court movement and stroke execution you can break down the problem posed by your opponent's shot into smaller, bite-size pieces.

The beginning tennis lesson gives you an idea of how to hit the ball without having to worry about the factors of varying ball height, ball speed, angle, court movement, etc. If the pro can stabilize how you hit your forehand under perfect conditions, he then attempts to teach you how to apply what is basically that same forehand to conditions where you have to run twenty feet to one side, bend your knees, hit the ball on the run and recover back into position toward the middle of the court.

The challenge is that when you start taking tennis lessons you may get the illusory feeling that you are a fairly good player because you can now consistently hit back that easily tossed, perfectly lofted ball that the pro feeds you. Of course, you never see such a nice ball again when you try to play with your friends. Hence the attraction of a ball machine for new students. As a beginner, if you have a beginner friend, you are pretty poor practice for each other. You will probably create all sorts of new, erroneous stroke patterns trying to deal with the fact that the ball never is in the right place. Unless you take turns just tossing the ball to each other.

The tennis pro who understands this syndrome will naturally address the next level of development of the player, which is that the player needs to learn how to recreate the pristine experience of the "perfect" tennis stroke in the complex situation of actual court play.

What the tennis player faces is a constant improvisational give and take between what constitutes his "perfect" forehand and the situation at hand. The ideal conditions are as follows: The ball comes to you at a comfortable speed, right in the middle of your normal swing zone, you have ample time to hit it, your feet are in perfect position, and you swing away.

The situation at hand, what you actually face on court, can be modified tremendously. The ball may be coming far faster, which cuts down on your comfort level, decreases the time you have to get your racket and your feet in position, and perhaps the height of the ball forces you to modify your stroke in some way. If you are a beginning player, you will probably abandon your instructed stroke and improvise something, anything, to hit the ball.

A better player systematically breaks down the complex situation that he faces, and often arrives at the ball anyway with plenty of time to hit the clean forehand that he learned from his original instructor. So many habits of the better player contribute to making his life much easier than the beginner. "You make it look so easy," they are told. But the casual observer of the superior player misses crucial behaviors that enable that easy-looking shot.

Most of these behaviors happen in the gap of time between the shots. As it turns out, despite the obvious importance of having a good tennis stroke, most of what makes a successful player is not so much how he hits the ball, but what he does when he is not hitting the ball, i.e. - in the gap between the strokes.

There are a number of "between the strokes" factors that contribute to simpler, trimmer, more executable shots by putting the hitter under less challenging conditions. The following are some of the things you can do "in the gap." There are probably many more of these. This will give you a good start. And they all qualify as point projects.

From now on in this book, if I suggest a point project, I'll number it based on what stroke it corresponds to, as **F-1** for the first forehand tip, **S-4** for the fourth serve tip, etc. (**G** will stand for "In the Gap").

First of all, preparation for your stroke may have started several shots back. Like a pool player, but without the luxury of the time available to the pool shark for deliberation, you may have hit a shot with the hopes of setting up an even more devastating shot. For example, you may serve wide to the deuce court, hit the next shot to the open court and close in to the net to volley. That is playing a point with a plan. If you can dictate the flow of play in this way, you naturally have an advantage: you know what is coming. If you know what is coming, the likelihood that you will be in the right place at the right time is increased tremendously.

Most people prepare for their next shot after the other person hits the ball. That may seem like a logical time to start. After all, how can you know what to do until the other person has hit the ball? But the skilled player may have a whole list of things he does way before the other person hits the ball and while he is hitting the ball, in addition to what he does after the opponent actually hits the ball. It's in this "way before and during" category that a tremendous amount of improvement can be made in most people's game play.

I described above how you may prepare for the shot several hits earlier. Still, the fundamental punctuation point for beginning your shot is immediately after your last shot. The first thing is to

G-1: reestablish your balance and optimal court position.

If you have hit a shot that can be followed up to the net, you hustle in a few steps. If you have hit a shot off to one side of the court, you drift or quickly recover back toward the center of the court. The latter action is of course influenced by where you hit your last shot.

For example, if you, a right handed player, ran over to the forehand side of the court and hit the ball cross court, you obviously shouldn't stand and lovingly watch your ball float over the net. Anyone with a brain, two legs and a forehand will be scorching you down the line to your backhand in about two seconds. But, even so, you don't recover from your crosscourt shot all the way to the center of the court. You recover to about one meter to the right of the center mark on the back line. That's because you can't run all the way back to the middle after hitting a crosscourt shot, or you too will be chasing down a crosscourt.

Even so, despite such a detailed analysis, you do immediately "repair" your court position and your stance to what is commonly called a ready position. This may happen after you scurry up to the net a bit, but you still straighten things up, if you can, to something that approximates two feet spread apart about shoulder width, racket held in front of the body, ready to move in response to your opponent's next stroke.

Another pre-stroke behavior, i.e. - before your opponent's stroke, is watching the ball. Most people start watching the ball after their opponent hits it. You always hear that, "eye on the ball" or, "watch the ball." But what many people don't know is that you can start to

G-2: watch the ball BEFORE your opponent hits it.

This is most useful in the serve return, but the

technique can be applied to any stroke with good effect.

You can see why this would be so effective on the serve return. If you start watching the ball as it leaves the server's hand, you immediately establish the connection between your eye and the ball. This connection is crucial. I have a feeling that many people only pick up the ball visually on the serve return a few feet before it clears the net on its way into your face. In that situation, you hardly have any time to respond to the direction of the ball and get your racket on it.

The experience of watching the ball as it leaves my serving opponent's hand gives me a feeling that the ball is MY ball, and that the serve is only the ball bouncing off a wall somewhere, as if I had hit it. This "I hit their serve" feeling is surprising but unmistakable. Since I was watching the ball before they hit it, I'm aware of the direction that their ball takes off of their racket at a much earlier stage, and I can react that much more quickly.

The next level of "gap" behavior (in the gap between the strokes) has to do with observations that you can make about the opponent's stroke during the stroke. If they are serving, you may note how they toss the ball or their racket preparation in order to get clues about what kind of a serve they are going to hit. If they toss the ball back over their head it is more likely to be a highly spinning, curving serve, rather than a hard, flat serve. On a groundstroke, you may see how they are preparing their racket for the stroke, their foot and body position, or you may have learned something from watching what they have done in similar situations in the past. In any case, you want to

G-3: watch them hit the ball.

Then there is your behavior during their stroke. In a way you can look at hitting with another person as a kind of a dance. What that means is that you react to all of the movements of your opponent as if you were one unit. You move when you hit the ball, you move when they hit the ball. The ideal movement that many pros are suggesting during the other person's shot is the split step.

If you can take a little hop during their hit, or even just as they take their racket back for their hit, split your feet onto your toes on a shoulder-width base, and then take off from that base in the direction of their ball, you often find yourself getting to the next ball faster. This

G-4: split step during their hit

is not always as easy as it seems. For example, you've just blistered your serve in, you're charging the net, and it doesn't seem like a great time to pause and split.

But it is, because nothing is more delightful for your opponent to hit against than a moving target. If I'm settled quickly in a ready position, my opponent has a lot more work to do than if I am running ferociously in some direction, one foot occasionally on the ground, unable to stop and change directions.

The split step punctuates the point. It says "I hit my serve, move in (and split while you hit), I move to your next ball, hit it, take some territory toward the net or recover court position, (and split while you hit), etcetera. Many points are lost by coming in too close to the net after the serve. Yes, you want to get in. But you can get in a couple of steps after your serve, and maybe a couple more while you move in to the next ball, but to get six steps in and then have to hit a half-volley at your feet on the dead run is suicidal, at least in terms of your desire to win the point.

After they have hit the ball, you enter into another major phase of "gap" behavior. The first thing that we should do is start eliminating variables. Our dream is to eliminate so many variables that the final result will be our shot executed in a manner as calm and pristine as the shot hand-fed to you by your personal tennis pro. The pro tries to make it as easy for you as possible. It's your job on court to do the same for yourself, to whatever degree you can.

To do that, you speed up your actions in the gap between the strokes. The first movement that most people make, intuitively, is toward the ball that your opponent hit. But that is not what the best players do. They start eliminating things that keep them from being able to hit the ball properly. And they establish the things they need, in order of priority. And, as bizarre as it sounds, the first priority is not to be standing where the ball is hit to return the ball. It's important, but not as important as racket preparation.

Try making your shoulder turn and racket preparation your number one priority.

G-5: Turn your shoulder first, and then move to the ball.

By doing that you automatically get your shoulder turned, and have your racket in a position that it can at least do something. A turned body can run in the direction of the ball, not just skip sideways. You may not get your full shoulder turn, i.e. enough that they will be looking at your back as you hit (more on this to come), but at least you will have turned.

There are some unusual projects that I subject myself to in practice, hoping to establish an optimal timing relationship to the ball. For example, sometimes I make it my point project to

G-6: rise and fall with the ball,

in a kind of dance. That is, I make both my racket and my body rise and fall with the ball. What that means is that when the ball is rising on my opponent's shot as it clears the net, I'm rising, moving to the ball and my racket is rising as I take it back high in the air in a looping fashion. When the ball starts to fall down into my court I start to let my racket fall down toward the court (still in my hand, of course), I bend my knees, get down, and when the ball hits the ground my racket is at the lowest point in my swing. When the ball is down my racket is way down. When the ball starts to rise off the bounce my racket is rising again, and I straighten up my legs plus hit up through the rising ball from low to high, which again gives me control of the ball.

This timing pattern helps you hit balls that are rising

off of the bounce (which is after my little dance move) as well as falling, which is an advanced skill, plus giving you a sense of where your racket should be when the ball is in the air. Some people don't start their swing until the ball has bounced, which in the case of the rising ball is way too late. The thing that's interesting about the rising ball in comparison to the falling ball is that they both typically pass through your comfortable hitting zone. Both of them need to be hit in the same way: from low to high. It takes finer timing to hit the rising ball from below, but if you rise and fall with it and have your racket already low on the bounce of the ball, you'll be the one giving the ball the lesson, not vice versa.

Of course you can try the forehand like this, too, but on the backhand you need it even more, because unless you get ahead of the ball on the backhand you will probably just be slowly wearing out your side of the net rather than your opponent.

Another thing I work on sometimes is to

G-7: get the feet set by the time the ball bounces.

It may not always be possible, but if you go for early preparation like this, the more likely you will be totally set up and ready to whale on the ball.

Chapter 6

Point Projects for the Forehand

Beginner Projects:

Proper grip

The reason that the pro puts attention on your grip is that he has a particular stroke in mind that he is hoping that you will hit soon, and that stroke will not work without you holding the racket with a certain grip. Since people have been playing tennis for many years they have discovered that some things work better than others. For example, they have discovered that hitting the ball with a flat swing will simply send the ball long, out of the court. This is one reason untrained players think that tennis is a genteel, serene sport, because they can't hit the ball very hard or it will sail out of the court. No self-respecting adult male can stand pit-patting a ball back and forth when if he used his full strength he could hit it over the fence.

The pro has this in mind when she asks you to hold the

racket in a certain way. The proper grip is one element, that, when coupled with the proper stroke, will result in you being able to hit the ball as hard as you like and still have it land in the court.

The challenge is that the grip is typically different for different strokes. This requires that you change the grip just like you switch gears in a car. To do this you use the non-hitting hand to change from one grip to the other between strokes. This change has to become automatic.

The good news is that it will quickly become second nature. The bad news is that there is actually a lot more to this change than a simple grip change. To hit the ball properly, you will need not only to change the grip, but to set the racket in a particular relationship to your wrist and arm while you turn the body, run, get set, and then hit. What you really need to practice is not just the grip change but this change from one wrist angle to another. Of course, without the proper grip and the grip change you wouldn't be able to hit the ball from any angle.

Racket Back

Your pro will tell you to take your racket back but she probably doesn't mean it the way that it sounds. The racket is not the primary focus before the shot. The body is the primary thing that needs turning. When you turn the body, the racket goes along with it. You can leave the racket hanging comfortably at your side and still hit a powerful stroke, if you have a complete shoulder turn

Oddly, the ideal tennis groundstroke is not powered by the arm–it's powered by the rotation of the torso. I explain to my students that if you could hang a camera in the air a few feet off the end of the racket and have it follow the stroke, the only movement of the arm that it would detect would be the movement of the arm in the shoulder joint from low to high.

In the ideal stroke (my version), the arm does not move from front to back in the shoulder joint, only from down to up, because the forward motion of the racket is provided by the rotation of the body. This is the great failing of many beginning players, and the source of a lot of injuries. Hitting the ball forward with only an arm motion disengages the shot from it's most powerful energy source, hip and torso rotation, strangling that power transfer at the shoulder (or never engaging it in the first place) and puts the shoulder at risk for injury.

So when someone tells you, "racket back" what you should really hear is "turn the front shoulder away from the ball."

Low to High

The reason that your pro tells you this is that hitting a tennis ball requires that you clear the net and that you learn to add an element of control by spinning the ball end over end. The instant that a ball leaves your racket it becomes subject to the law of gravity and starts falling to the ground. If you hit a ball that is three feet off of the ground in a horizontal plane it will hit the ground at the same time as a ball dropped right by your racket. Since the net is three feet high at its lowest point you will never win points that way. Therefore you need to loft almost every ball for it to clear the net. This is best accomplished by hitting the ball from low to high rather than by adopting a particular angle of the wrist upon contact.

The element of topspin, i.e. a ball that is spinning end over end with the top edge proceeding toward your opponent's court, causes the ball to curve down and into their court. We have therefore, two reasons to hit up, one, to clear the net by a wide margin, and another, to bring that lofted ball back down into the court.

You might ask why we don't just hit it mostly flat and eliminate those conflicting forces, which makes sense except for the fact that a flat ball like that may only have a tiny margin for error to make it in the court. It may actually be impossible for a ball hit with the pace that a pro can generate to land in the court without topspin. When you consider that a ten-year-old child can hit the ball long and out, just imagine what a six foot seven Aussie can do.

The term low to high refers to your racket head. It's important to remember that "low to high" refers to the position of the racket in relation to the ball, not the ground. If you start the racket on the level of the ball as it is coming toward you, swing through and end high, you have not actually accomplished the intent of this phrase. You need to start (or get) the racket below the ball (low) and end with it high or above the ball. That will give you lift, topspin, control, and allow you to hit the ball as hard as you want and yet have it crank down into the opponent's court with pace, and even accelerate a little after it hits.

Hit out in front

We want to hit out in front because that is where we have the most power. As your body turns into the shot it doesn't maximize its full transfer of power until it gets in front of the body. So that's where we want to make contact. If you make this your top priority it will force you to modify the length of your backswing (i.e. - shoulder turn) and make sure that you are meeting the ball in the proper place. A hard hit ball may cause you to abbreviate your racket preparation (more on this later), but you don't want to compromise on this hitting out in front thing. Another reason that you need to hit out in front, again, is because the topspin shot that your pro is probably giving you will not work properly unless you make contact early.

Even if you are hitting a two handed backhand, which some pros teach, especially for younger and smaller players, you will still want to make contact out in front.

As you begin your warm up, practice each of these items in turn, focusing only on one point project at a time. You can keep working on that one project until you feel that you have it or just hit ten balls each, focusing on each, and then continue with your practice.

My Forehand Projects:

Looking at the forehand from beginning to end, there are many variables that contribute to success. There are, of course, many kinds of forehands that people hit, but the forehand that I will describe is a topspin forehand with a semi-western grip. Any pro will have a number of tips for the forehand, and this chapter will simply be a sample of some of the things that I look for in a good forehand. You may have other ideas or other information from your pro or from watching good players or from reading. These examples are just to get you started.

First of all, you can experiment quite a bit with the backswing of the racket. You can, as I have stated, eliminate the concept of backswing from your mind entirely. You can look at taking the racket back on the forehand as strictly a matter of turning your body away from the net, using an extreme shoulder turn.

Try this: stand up, arms at your side. Then reach out with your two hands in front of you at waist height, palms up, and grasp an imaginary barbell. Now look at your racket hand. If you replaced the imaginary barbell with an imaginary tennis handle sticking out of your racket hand at the same angle as the barbell, you would see how far back you have to take your tennis racket in relation to your body.

I think that you can visualize that the imaginary racket is automatically "back" just due to the angle that you are holding it in your hand. You don't have to take it back IN RELATION TO YOUR BODY any farther than that.

What you do have to do is turn your shoulders (and torso) away from the net to get that racket back farther. So, our first forehand point project is to

F-1: practice where to set the racket when you "take it back."

We don't have to take it very far back, because we make an extreme shoulder turn to get the racket back even farther. You can practice this without hitting any balls for a while, and then try ten balls with this clear racket setting behavior. Of course, your shoulder has to turn to get the racket there. One thing that makes this interesting is to set your racket in the instant you know where the ball is going. By doing that you are ready to hit and have only to move to the ball and execute your shot. Many people wait until they get to the ball to get their shot ready. Why wait? Get it done in the gap, make your life simple.

One thing that a lot of pros emphasize is the role of the non-dominant hand in most if not all tennis strokes. In the forehand, for a righty, it's important to get your left hand back, too. You don't want that left hand out there in front of you. You want it turning back with your right hand. The reason for this is that if you leave your left hand trailing behind while your right arm goes back, you have started to disconnect the arms from the torso. If

F-2: both arms go back,

the torso and the arms are a single unit, coiling back before unleashing a strike. If only one arm goes back, part of the torso's energy is not being packed tightly into an explosive force. It's hanging back to support a wayward arm that is as if out of the game.

I use a rather silly analogy on this one, but so what, if

it works? Let's say that the racket going back is the pancake, and your left hand going back with it is the pat of butter, trying to catch up with the pancake. Then you hurl your breakfast over to the other guy. Kind of a high carbohydrate forehand, I guess. Kids get the analogy. It's working, anyway, until I come up with another one.

Another thing that you can experiment with is the angle of the racket face when you "take it back." I find that I can get more topspin if I

F-3: get the racket face almost parallel to the ground on the backswing.

To stabilize this with tennis pupils I sometimes have them balance a ball on the backhand side of the racket before they hit their forehand. They wait with their racket back, I put a ball on it, and then I walk around in front of them and feed another ball to them to practice their "flatback" forehand. The balanced ball naturally falls off as they groove their forehand. This trains them to think of a flat racket in the back (like a pancake... see?).

The interesting thing about this shot is that I try to get them to start the stroke in the direction that the face of the racket is facing, i.e. - down. By starting the stroke down toward the ground they more naturally get the racket below the ball as it comes forward and can hit a topspin shot.

This is how I work with more introductory level players, but with an advanced player I would have them take the racket up much higher, pointing the flat racket face at the back wall of the court and then taking it even further back using a shoulder turn. This high back racket preparation coupled with the extreme shoulder turn, which I describe with the phrase

F-4: show them your back

adds the momentum of the falling racket to the power of the stroke and naturally helps guide the racket down below and up through the ball, which is the racket trajectory that we need in order to get topspin and take control of this powerful shot.

Obviously this is my big forehand, where I have plenty of time for such racket preparation. When I don't have time I may content myself with the pancake version, using that shot as a sort of counter-punch. But more on that later.

Regardless of the length of the stroke, I work hard to clarify the optimal racket trajectory as it hits that ball. The techniques that better tennis players have acquired over the years to gain control of the ball, although effective, are often counter-intuitive to the novice player. Tennis pros are often telling their students what to do, but sometimes they fail to tell them why. I like to explain the logic behind the instruction so that the student can see where we are going with the apparently bizarre instructions I'm suggesting.

For example, the obvious desire of the beginning player is to hit the ball. That makes sense. In order to do that, the player must match the flight of a ball through the air with the movement of a tennis racket through space, in opposing directions. Hence, the natural inclination of the new player is to do what I call "matching," i.e. - matching the height and path of the racket to the height and path of the ball. Since the major anxiety of the new player is about making contact with the ball at all, this makes total sense.

But that is not at all what the tennis pro typically wants you to do. The tennis pro is trying to help you build a game that will take you a long way. He knows that if you match the line of flight of the ball you will only be able to hit flat balls, and therefore you will never gain control over the ball. Your only element of control will be how hard you hit the ball. If you hit it too hard it will go out. But not with the spin shot that the pro is trying to graft on to you from day one.

Instead of matching the line of flight of the ball with your racket stroke, I suggest that you think of penetrating that line of flight from low to high. That, coupled with a proper grip, will result in a topspin ball, which allows for power and control. So, you have to visualize the actual path that the ball is taking through the air, and think of

F-5: bisecting the path of the ball with your racket,

sweeping up through the path of that ball from low to high.

Another analogy that I use is the idea that you are a giant and the ball when hit is as if resting on the top of a mountain in front of you, about waist high. In order to hit that ball properly for tennis you don't hit it with the flatter swing of the baseball player. You have to take your (giant, way oversize) tennis racket and swing up the valley before hitting the ball off the top of the mountain.

My mental abbreviation for this is

F-6: "valley up!"

What that brings to mind (for me anyway), is that before I hit every ball, I have to create an imaginary valley in the air before I make contact. That guarantees that I will get topspin. Hitting serve returns like this I almost never miss. It's a mental reminder that you don't just match the height of the incoming ball, hoping to get it back. You literally put your own spin on the situation. That's what makes you the master of the ball, rather than the opposite.

It might seem that this is a bit silly, but this is actually one of the most useful tips that I personally use in both counterpunching and serve return situations, because it reminds me that I need to get the racket below the ball and hit up, not just hit through the ball.

I also work on getting the legs into the shot. I find that this has an almost miraculous effect on my consistency. I like to look at the relationship between the ball and the player as a continual student versus teacher role-reversal struggle. Who's going to be the teacher? Is the ball going to teach you or are you going to teach the ball? Are you the master or the student? One thing that clearly distinguishes a teacher from a student is that the teacher has a plan before stepping on the court. This, in a larger sense, is how you can change your self from a passive learner to an active learner, which is of course the theme of this book.

One thing that characterizes the situation where you are imposing your plan on the ball rather than vice versa is if you have bent your knees to get below the ball. We want your stroke to come up from low to high through the ball ("valley up"). But how can you hit up on a ball that is too low? No way, unless you modify your stroke. But we don't want you to modify your stroke. That is the behavior of a beginner. As we discussed, he has a new stroke for every ball that comes over the net.

If you

F-7: bend your knees and get below every ball,

and straighten out your knees on the hit, you almost always get to hit your standard topspin forehand. If the ball is a low ball, you are already down there for it. If it's a higher ball, the straightening of your legs brings you up through the ball and adds power and more topspin to your shot. In that case, you got up earlier in the morning than the ball, you got down, got there early and made the ball take the lesson (over to the other side, making someone else into the student).

I heard once that one of the distinguishing factors of really great tennis players is that they all have powerful legs. This was one of McEnroe's secret weapons. If you don't have strong legs you might want to put some work in at the gym, with some lunges and maybe get into Pilates or something to enhance your leg strength. It's no joke trying to get the full power of your legs into even one stroke, not to mention every stroke, including serves, all day long. Feel the burn in practice, or you'll have lukewarm results when you play.

Another big forehand thing is to

F-8: hit out in front.

I discussed this in detail in the beginner section, but I didn't want to forget to mention it here.

These are just a few forehand tips. There are many more and many competing theories of the forehand. But this gives you a taste of my version.

Chapter 7.

Point Projects for the Backhand

For the Beginner:

Certainly much of what has been said about the forehand applies to the backhand.

Your pro will have shown you a different grip for the backhand, which we have already discussed means a completely different angle of the racket to the arm, as well.

I would like to encourage you that in some ways the backhand motion is a more natural motion for the body, when it's done properly. There is no reason why the backhand can't be your best stroke, or even your most powerful stroke. A two handed backhand can certainly be a formidable weapon.

The famous saying about Ginger Rogers is that she could dance just as well as Fred Astaire, but she did it all backwards and on high heels. Just like that you still need a proper grip, your racket back (shoulder turn), a low to high stroke, and hitting out in front, but you need to do it on the other side of the body.

Just remember that Ginger was the good-looking one.

My Backhand Projects:

Backhands and forehands are like men and women. They're the same species, similar in many ways, but still totally different. Looking at the backhand brings out a number of point projects similar to the forehand, but with some crucial differences. Most obviously we are hitting on the other side of the body. That changes things in some non-obvious ways. For example, with a one handed backhand, our hitting arm is obviously closer to the net when the ball arrives, because it's attached to the front shoulder this time instead of the back one.

The only area where you can expect to get a ball back on your (one handed) backhand is in front of your body. On the forehand it's possible that you can still get the ball back even after it has penetrated the air space in front of your chest all the way back to the shoulder farthest from the net, but on the backhand such a ball would be almost past hope. Therefore, we have to be even more aware of the importance of

B-1: hitting out in front.

If hitting out in front is your number one priority rather than your last priority, everything else must be adjusted in order to accomplish that task.

For example, you may

B-2: shorten up your backswing if you are rushed

on the stroke so that you can be sure to hit the ball way out in front. You are then hitting a counter-punching shot that gets the ball back but probably doesn't have any aggressive damage-causing potential. And consider the abundance of situations that happen in which you may be "rushed." They could hit the ball harder than you expected. It could be a very deep ball that you will have little time to hit. You could have to hit the ball on the rise. You could be hitting a serve return. And (a very frequent situation), you could be hitting the ball during or just after running cross-court.

In all of those situations you can shorten up your backswing and just take the last two thirds of your stroke. You need to keep your traditional follow through to retain the control element that that brings to your stroke.

What this long list of counterpunching situations means is that it is rare that you actually get to hit your big, full swinging backhand (or forehand). Only when you didn't have to run, aren't rushed, and not hitting a serve return do you get to hit your big shot. That's not a lot of the time.

Let's go through the sequence of actions on the backhand. Like the forehand, you are going to

B-3: turn your shoulders first and run with your shoulders turned.

B-4: The non-dominant hand should support the racket

during this turning and running. This has the double benefit of stabilizing the racket during turning and running, plus also guaranteeing that you get a good shoulder turn and don't just take the racket back with the arm.

As a beginner you want to emphasize

B-5: set the head of the racket low on the backswing

so that it is already below the line of flight of the incoming ball. This is also very effective on serve returns. More advanced players may want to experiment with a "broken" elbow technique, which adds phenomenal pace to the ball.

This is a Sampras specialty, (and Gustavo Kuerten) where on his backhand he'll take the racket back with his upper arm pointing straight out from his shoulder but with the

B-6: elbow bent.

When he hits the ball he brings the racket head down from that position, gaining great momentum, looping down below the incoming line of flight of the ball and then coming up with great force to hit the ball with power and increased topspin. That is an advanced technique, however, and until you stabilize the basic backhand, I would suggest that you might wait to add Pete and Guga's special shot to your list of weapons.

I also try to hit the backhand with a valley-up motion, as described in the forehand chapter, hitting the ball off the top of the mountain, but this is just one of many analogies.

The point is that you have to

B-7: get below the ball.

The "Sampras/Guga Special" backhand naturally tends to drop the racket below the ball, but with or without that shot, you need to get below the ball on your hit, because you have to lift the ball over the net.

It's very important on the backhand to both get below the ball and to hit it out in front. The reason is that when you take your racket back on the backhand, the front face of the racket naturally tends to face downwards toward the court. What that means is that unless you get your racket out in front, way further out in front than on the forehand, your racket face is going to be angled down toward the court too far on contact, which will hit your ball in the net.

As a matter of fact, this gives you an instant diagnosis. If your backhands are going in the net, it's highly likely that you are hitting them too late, too close to your body, and therefore there is no way they could get the lift they need to clear the net. So, focus on the hit out in front (**B-1**) point project and you'll usually see instant results.

Timing is crucial here. To make sure that you are ahead of the ball, you have to time things properly.

As I said, if the ball gets ahead of me, the ball is the teacher and I'm the student. If I'm ahead of the ball, I'm the teacher and the ball is the student. I want to be in control of the little encounter, where I'm giving the lesson and the ball is obediently flying over the net back where it belongs. "Ahead of the ball" for me means that I have my racket back in plenty of time, and that I get lower than the ball. It's the corollary to the early bird gets the worm analogy: If the racket gets below the ball, the racket takes control. If the ball gets below the racket, the ball takes control and tends to make you to hit down, usually into the net.

Don't forget that you should

B-8: show them your back

if you have managed to get your feet set and have time, because that will mean that your torso will get into the shot and you will hit one scorching backhand.

There are a few schools of thought on the finish of the backhand. One school says that you should come up with the arm with the motion that you would use to

B-10: open a window shade.

Others will say that you should bring the racket up and let it cross in front of the body like a windshield wiper. The point of the latter is to free the racket to swing away through the ball (upward) creating phenomenal topspin. Others allow the wrist to release through the ball and upward.

Personally, I'm working with the latter two, often in combination. Whatever you do, focus on it solely for enough point project strokes to stabilize what your personal backhand shot is going to be.

Chapter 8

Point Projects for the Serve

For the Beginner:

The serve is a complicated motion, but it is not, hopefully, an alien one. It is fundamentally the same as throwing a ball. If you have never learned how to throw a ball you would do well to practice that motion for some time before trying to serve. One of the sure signs of ball-throwing deficiency is the person who does not turn his shoulder away from the targeted party and tries to do the whole thing with their arm.

This type of throw is the origin of the phrase, "you throw like a girl." The phrase is really a misnomer, since the only real meaning underlying the expression is that the party in question throws like someone who either was never trained to throw or never cared to learn.

I've taught many a male player who couldn't serve their way out of a paper bag, and, sure enough, when you took the racket out of their hand and asked them to simply throw a ball, they were as clueless as any pair of X chromosomes has ever been.

Joe Namath, famous for his football throwing (and other) abilities, would turn his back away from the target and then uncoil a smoothly thrown missile. People said that he had a natural throwing motion. The irony is that it was simply what his college coach told him to do.

If you have an old racket that you don't care about, you could practice throwing it across a field, just to get a sense of this motion. And then take a lesson.

Another thing that might help you is to learn to juggle, or at least practice tossing the ball with your non-dominant hand for quite a while. The serve is the only shot where we personally control the location where we hit the ball. Of course that control element is compromised if we can't come up with a consistent toss with another hand than the one that we have typically ever tossed a ball with. So, practice, practice, practice.

My Serve Projects:

The serve is like a finely oiled machine. It has a lot of parts, and they all have to be working properly or it falls apart. Or it may work but not as powerfully or efficiently as it could. I work on the parts one by one, and hope that the whole thing adds up to something great. Sometimes it does.

I'll mention a few point projects on the serve, starting with what happens first. First of all I have a shoulder turn. I say to my students,

S-1: "show them your back".

I've said that on forehands and backhands too, of course. That means you turn your back as far away from the other person as you can on the backswing. You don't just throw up the ball and hit it, you throw it up and coil your body back, away from the ball, so you gain the power of your torso rotation to help you powder the ball. Your rotated torso is far more powerful than your arm. We are trying to harness that power on all of our strokes so you can hit with more power and less arm effort.

When I turn I also

S-2: bend the knees.

What that does is get you below the ball (again), so that you can hit up on it with explosive force. The serve can be very challenging to hit because it is both the hardest and one of the shortest shots in the game. You are able to hit the ball harder than any other shot, but it must curve down and land in the court much sooner than any other ball, because you have to hit on the half of your opponent's court that is closest to the net. You want incredible pace but also great control. That means that you may need even more topspin on this shot than on any other shot. Getting your knees bent before the shot adds an extra amount of low to high contact to the ball, and gives you more topspin, plus adding the explosive power of your legs to the torso rotation power that you have already stored up.

The toss is my next item of consideration. I think that the toss is one of the most neglected and yet most important aspects of the serve. Since you toss the ball yourself, you are fundamentally in control of the ball, unlike any other shot in the game. However, as I said, if you can't throw the ball up in a consistent fashion, this advantage is erased. So, I actually

S-3: practice the toss.

I might get out there and try five to ten tosses before I even hit a ball. This is even more important in windy conditions, where your ball gets blown all over.

I also use the toss as an "instant" cure for a number of serving problems. If you stick your racket straight up in the air with your arm straight and then move it a little bit farther forward toward the net, naturally the face of the racket will start to angle downwards toward the net. If you raise the racket back to vertical and then move it farther back, the racket face will start to angle up toward the sky. This gives us a natural cure for "length" problems on your serve. There are only two length problems: short or long.

The short serve, i.e. - the serve that goes into the net, has an instant cure: toss the ball 4-6 inches farther back. That naturally takes the trajectory of the ball higher, and it will in all likelihood clear the net. The long serve is curable by a toss that is farther forward. The long serve also benefits from a good deal of topspin, but the toss cure can help. This idea of self-diagnosis and self-cure is very important in tennis, since you're alone out there, usually with no coaching.

Another thing that I emphasize on the toss that I don't hear a lot of other people talking about is that

S-3: the toss should be on the side of your body.

The fact is that your arm is on one side of your body, not sticking out of the top of your head (we hope so, anyway). That means that if you are using torso rotation on your serve, your arm will naturally be coming around on (for a righty) the right side of your body. Why not toss the ball over there on the right so that you can hit it there? So many people toss the ball straight over their heads or straight in front and wonder why they have no power. A toss straight over your head doesn't take advantage of all of the angular or rotational momentum that your body can generate. So, toss to the side, rotate your torso and you'll unleash an animal serve.

One thing that you still need to remember is to

S-4: watch the ball.

I believe that if I asked most people where the serve is hit they would say "into the service box." But that's where the serve is hit to, i.e. – the target of the serve. The serve is actually hit up and to the side of the body. So that is where you should be looking when you serve. If you give your full attention to the location of the ball in the air, you hit it with more force and certainty. In addition, this focused attention gives you more facility when you attempt to hit slice and twist serves, since you are simply changing the spin that you are applying to a ball that is only a foot or so from your head. The hit happens where you are, not over the net. Keep your focus on the ball until the shot is hit.

S-5: drop behind your back.

Most effective serves are hit with a drop of the racket behind your back just before hitting up to the ball. This drop adds significant power and also topspin. People who have trouble with this drop and with the torso rotation mentioned above, often simply don't even know how to throw a ball. When I find someone with an unusual service motion I just hand them a ball, see if they can throw it, and usually discover that they don't have a clue how to perform that basic task. I sometimes just teach them how to throw and then move them into serving. I often dream of padding a tennis racket with foam so that the student could get the idea of throwing the racket over the net as a natural precursor to hitting the ball with the same motion. Someday I'll do it.

The drop behind the back isn't just a basic task on the serve; it also gives you an element of variety. I find that a more extreme drop behind the back adds more topspin on the ball, which brings it down in to the court. This is a natural motion for a second serve, or just to mix up the action of the ball so that your opponent doesn't get your timing memorized.

On the other hand, sometimes I work with just getting the elbow of my hitting arm up high on the backswing and simply letting the momentum of the shoulder turn into the hit make the racket fall into the drop behind the back. Keeping the elbow high on the backswing seems to keep your arm loose to release a lot of power into the ball. This is also how I hit the overhead (more on that to come).

For an advanced player, you need to get a lesson on

S-6: pronation,

which is allowing your wrist to follow through after the hit into a position where you could look at your watch on the back of your arm. This allows the racket to snap through the ball, adding 5-10 miles per hour to the serve. That's good. Sometimes you can practice just this component of your serve, holding your racket high in the air and just hitting it with pronated wrist action.

Another thing to remember on the serve is to

S-7: hold the racket loosely

in the hand. Vic Braden sometimes will have people practice serving with only three fingers (plus the thumb) on the racket, just to give that feeling of a looser grip. We want a relaxed grip because we want a relaxed wrist. With a looser racket in the hand, the whipping motion of the drop behind the back plus pronation can really kick the ball over the net. Once you get the feeling of that loose racket down, you can go back to all four fingers.

The whip analogy is a good one for the serve. A whip

is wide at the beginning and tiny at the tip. The serve starts with the wide hip and torso energy that your back gets going. That energy whips up into the narrower arm and racket, finishing with the final, relatively tiny (in comparison with the torso) action of your pronated wrist, which all together creates a highly accelerated serve.

I must admit to constantly tinkering with my serve, adding a little of this, a little of that. I get ideas for things that might make it faster, more challenging, or more reliable. All of this testing can result in usable techniques to help my game.

It might seem unusual to be finding new things like this to try out, but it makes perfect sense to me. First of all, tennis is an evolving sport, which is obvious to anyone who has watched the forehand grip slowly sneaking clockwise around the racket in the last 40 years. My brother stated hitting a high looping topspin forehand just for fun in 1960 and then started burning through the junior tournaments in his age group. Now everyone does it.

Even though there are established techniques for doing things, I don't believe everything has been invented yet. So, I keep experimenting. One thing that I have been tried out with successful results is an unusual racket preparation motion on the serve.

This is how it works: when I toss the ball and take my racket back, I don't stop the upswing of the arms at shoulder height. I take them up higher. Many people will toss the ball from about shoulder height, and when they bring the racket up on the backswing preparation for the serve, bend the elbow at about shoulder height and drop the head of the racket behind their back.

I do the same thing, basically, but I bring my arms up to a more vertical position before I let go of the ball and before dropping the racket back behind my back. To visualize the difference here, think of the difference between the upraised arms on the serve resembling the goalposts on an American football field and (my way) having them resemble an upraised "V" shape.

The effect of this is twofold. The toss in this scenario is shorter. It may only be about eight inches from the highest point that I can reach on this toss and the center of my upraised racket in the serve hitting position. This has the benefit of less airtime for the ball, which means that it should be more consistently placed, and, in windy conditions, have less time to get blown away.

The effect on the serve of this

S-8: high backswing

is a subjective feeling of openness, looseness, of more whipping motion popping into the serve, since it falls from higher in the air, and that momentum seems to transmit itself into the shot.

This gives me two serves off of the same racket preparation. The power serve is hit with the high preparation and a good shoulder turn, letting the natural fall of the racket and turn of the shoulder pop the ball with force over the net. The spin serve starts the same way, but I emphasize a deeper drop behind the back, which, when falling from so high, creates momentum for a tremendous upward hit on the back of the ball, forcing it to curve down into the court.

The value of this effect is getting the ball high over the net and still having it sink sharply down and make contact with the court before the service line. Since the net is the first obstacle of concern in tennis, having the ability to hit a serve that clears the net by some distance is great, as long as it can still sink down to bounce in the service box.

This is one of my tennis discoveries, which works for my serve and my game. You may try it and like it. Or you may make your own discoveries that are more suited for your particular physiology and temperament.

It's an odd thing, because on one hand we want you to learn the traditional strokes and apply them. But if you want to be your own best tennis pro, you need to think like a pro, and a good pro is not just parroting what he or she learned from someone else. The true professional is adding what she's learned and experienced to a natural curiosity, plus a consideration of the student's individual capabilities, and coming up with creative ways of expanding your tennis experience.

The only major difference between you and a professional is the time and attention that they have put into the sport. You can start to catch up, and at least be a useful contributor to your ongoing growth as a player, if you start to take on the attitude of a curious, resourceful, and even innovative student of the game.

Chapter 9

Point Projects for the Serve Return

For the Beginner:

The serve return, in some ways, should be your favorite groundstroke. You know, in general, where the ball is going to land, since it has to land in a much smaller space than any other stroke. You probably won't have to run over and hit it. Considering that your opponents will probably not be very advanced players, you shouldn't be getting serves with tremendous pace or spin, either.

Still, this stroke is not necessarily the normal, perfect forehand or backhand that you've been taught, but rather a shortened version of that shot. All you will really need to do is to turn your shoulders and hit the ball as you've been instructed, but without much in the way of racket "backswing." You can cut off the first third of your standard shot, but still finish the shot as usual. That will give you something to start with.

My Serve Return Projects:

The serve return is one of the most crucial and yet least practiced shots in the game. It's estimated that 50% of all shots are serves and serve returns. Most people practice their groundstrokes, some will practice their serve, but very few practice their serve return. People may think, "It's just a groundstroke." Which is of course true by definition, but it is also in many ways unlike a typical groundstroke.

First of all, it should be a much shorter stroke, if you are receiving a serve from anyone with a reasonable degree of pace on the ball. If you chopped off the first third of your normal groundstroke backswing and just started there, finishing with a normal follow-through, you might have a pretty good serve return. This serve return can be done by simply getting your shoulders turned and your racket out to the side from which position you finish out the stroke that you normally hit.

Just like the groundstroke, the serve return process starts very early. It starts when your opponent throws up the ball, when you

R-1: watch that toss.

It continues with a

R-2: shoulder turn as soon as you detect which side the ball is going to.

This shoulder turn moves your racket to the

appropriate side of the body. At that point you may have to hit the ball right away. Usually you don't need more turn to add additional power because all of the power you need is already available in the kinetic energy provided by your opponent's serve. You just reflect it back to him

Once you have made your turn, if you are hitting a topspin shot, you need to focus on

R-3: getting the racket below the ball

and hitting up through it. Remember that tennis is a lifting game (thank-you, Vic Braden), and that the first obstacle is the net. You don't have much time on the serve return, so you need to get the basics straight. The other thing to remember is to

R-4: hit the ball out in front.

Hitting the ball out in front has several major advantages. You are stronger out in front than you are to the side, so when you hit out in front you are more in your power zone.

Hitting out in front is important for visual tracking reasons, too. The ball that gets to your side has suddenly changed in your line of vision. For seventy feet it has been flying through the air toward you from one direction in relationship to your body, and now you are going to try to hit it on the side of your body, where it only lingers for a microsecond. It's easier to hit it and track it where you have already been watching it - out in front, before it moves off to your side and takes on a completely new angle.

One thing you can do to practice the serve return is have someone stand on the opposite service line and hit serves at you. Have them choke up on the racket and just whack the ball into your service box from there, using a snapping wrist motion on the racket. This is less tiring for them and has the advantage of getting the ball to you very rapidly. In that way, you groove your serve return to be an exceptionally compact stroke, and when they go back to hit real serves, it seems like you have a year to get the ball back. It's always better to plan for and train with less time. You can always adjust to more.

I'm constantly experimenting with new grips and coming up with new ideas for the serve return, but the main things that help are having a short backswing, getting my shoulder rather than just my arm around, penetrating the line of flight of the ball from low to high, and hitting out in front.

Don't forget the

R-5: split step during their toss,

and to

R-6: watch the ball all the way to the racket.

If I have a lot of time on the serve return, I may go ahead and hit my full normal groundstroke. But usually having a lot of time means that they have a soft serve and you can just as well use your short backswing to hit the ball on the way to the net. This short backswing shot doubles as a counterpunch when the point is underway and they are pushing you by hitting hard or by moving you around the court, and also can be used as an approach shot on a short ball.

One little secret that I have (or used to have until I told you) is to practice my serve return in the warm-up phase of a match when they are at the net and I am at the baseline. That way you are getting the ball hit to you quickly and you can practice your quick serve return.

Another thing to remember on the serve is that even though you want an abbreviated backswing, you still want a

R-7: full finish on the stroke

The reason for this is that your normal follow-through is still necessary in order to apply spin and control to the ball.

Another important thing is to

R-8: have a target

on your serve return. When they are serving it is easy to become passive and just react to what they do. Of course you do need to react properly... they hit first, that's why the serve is considered an advantage. But you can take some of their initiative away, at least psychologically, by watching the ball during the toss, as if taking possession of the ball in your vision and in your own mind, and then it seems as if to simply bounce off their racket according to your plan.

Then you take away their planning initiative on the serve because you hit the ball to the target that you have pre-selected. You can make many decisions. The most basic ones are 1) I'm going to hit cross court, 2) I'm going to hit down the line 3) I'm going to hit to the side of the court that he serves to me on - on my right side I'll hit right, on my left, left. 4) I'm going to switch sides, my right side crossing to his right (assuming a righty against righty), my left side crossing to his left.

These are general plans. You might come up with other ideas depending on whether they are left-handed or not, rushing the net on serve or not, can handle lobs or not, etc. Mix it up, but have a plan. That can put you back in charge of the point. It also gets rid of making the decision process of where to hit the ball during your return and you can simply focus on your stroke. You may have to abandon your plan if they do something wild, but it's good to start out with one.

Good luck, and watch the ball, all the way home.

Chapter 10

Point Projects for the Overhead

For the Beginner:

This shot is obviously similar to the serve, so it won't do you much good to learn this one first. Once you have stabilized the serve to some degree, the overhead will be easier to acquire. In some ways this shot is easier than the serve, since you don't need to toss the ball yourself and the shot is typically hit way closer to the net, giving you a greater margin for error for clearing the net. In addition you have the whole opposite court to hit into, rather than just the service box.

If you learn to love the overhead and hit it well, you will have a secret weapon that will surprise your opponent and put him at a tactical and psychological disadvantage.

My Overhead Projects:

I break the overhead into four main pieces, and execute each in turn:
1. Racket up
2. Move
3. Set
4. Hit

When I say

O-1: racket up

I mean I take my racket up in the air, my non-hitting arm in the air, and turn my shoulder, all in one motion. This mimics the unusual configuration that I described earlier in discussing the serve. The first result of this is readiness. Just like every other stroke that I have discussed in this book, I make my first task getting my racket ready to hit. If my racket isn't ready to hit it does me no good to run over to the ball.

The second element of this is that instead of waiting to hit with the racket dropped behind my back as is typical of most players, I have both arms virtually straight up in the air, with the racket head pointed at the sky. My non-hitting hand traces the path of the ball in the air, as if I was going to catch it with that hand. As a matter of fact that is a good practice project, simply having someone hit a number of lobs to you, which you will catch with your non-hitting hand. My racket hand floats poised above my head, waiting to go into action.

Then I

O-2: Move

to get myself in position to hit the ball. I always keep the ball in front of me, and like a baseball player I use my non-hitting hand to guide me to where the ball is going. It's said that if you extend this arm forward and up at a 45-degree angle you can use it to estimate the depth of the lob that you are receiving, since a ball falling below your pointing arm will require that you move forward, while a ball moving beyond the pointer will require that you move back. While I'm moving my racket is always in place, ready to hit.

Then I get

O-3: set

Which means that I have committed myself to a position where I believe I can hit the ball, out in front of me. Unless you get set you will have no firm base from which to launch a shot.

Then I

O-4: hit

Which simply means that I turn my shoulder toward the ball, and let my racket fall from its high position down to a drop behind my back, then surging up to hit the ball and follow through. If you want to get some real pop on this overhead you can of course pronate the wrist just like you did in your new service motion.

This of course is just my version of the overhead. Others may tell you something different. But I've found that this "falling" racket overhead gains tremendous power from the shoulder turn and is itself easy to execute. And powerful.

There is a lot more to be considered on this shot, such as the leaping overhead, typically hit when you can't get back far enough to get set. Plus the matter of where you should hit the shot (try to clear the net by at least two racket widths). But even so, you can start by breaking this shot down into the four pieces and practicing them separately, then reassembling them as a finished weapon.

To do that you simply have someone hit you a series of volleys at the net and occasionally throw up a lob. The latter action should cause you to immediately get your racket and nonhitting hand up, turn to the side and get set. First do this and don't even try to hit the ball, just let it bounce beside you. Then you can do the same thing and move, get set, and catch the ball in your nonhitting hand. This trains you to be in the proper position before hitting. Then try the whole thing.

Execute these four things, in order, and you will have a big, consistent overhead.

Chapter 11

Point Projects for the Volley

For the Beginner:

The volley should be your friend. Don't get caught in that "afraid of the ball" thing. There are many reasons why you should make friends with the volley:

1. It is technically easier to hit than the groundstroke.

2. The volley protects you from the ball

3. When you come up to the net you have a far superior set of angles to hit the ball into and can move your opponent all over the place

4. A bad volley can be better than a good groundstroke, just because you are in a better position

5. Hitting from up at the net gets the ball back to

the other guy much faster than almost any ball that you can hit from the baseline.

Many pros will start by teaching you the volley, just so that you learn how to make good contact with the ball and so that you will think of volleys as a normal shot. You'll also need this shot for doubles play, which is quite a bit of fun.

My Volley Projects:

You need a lesson on the volley. It's not just whaling on the ball. The volley is completely different than the groundstroke. It's a short, punching motion. You don't swing at it, in most circumstances.

The main thing to understand about the volley is that you want to make it as simple as possible. You want to get your racket in position quickly and punch forward into the ball with a compact motion. To understand what your tennis pro means when she says punch the volley, put your racket down, turn like a boxer so that the shoulder of your non-dominant hand is closer to your imaginary opponent, and then shadow box a punch with your dominant hand. Notice what happens. Your fist starts the punch close to your body and extends out in front of your body. As you extend out to punch, your shoulder may turn to give your punch more reach.

Now turn your body so that the shoulder of your dominant hand is closest to your imaginary sparring partner. Now punch. That punch, extending out on the backhand side, is called a jab. You can't turn your shoulder with the punch because your shoulder is already closest to the opponent.

Either way, this is one of the popular methods of teaching the volley. There are many other schools of thought on this (and every other) stroke. In any case, remember that on the punch volley your fist starts out close to your head. The same thing is true on the volley. Vic Braden (again) will say, "it's like you want to take a bite out of the ball," but you punch it instead. So, you get your head close to the ball before the volley.

The other thing to remember about the volley is that you

V-1: Aim the shot for the entire shot.

What that means is that you immediately line up the face of the racket to aim at the target where you hope to hit the ball and you move the racket crisply forward straight in the direction that you hope the ball will go, and at the end of your stroke, even after the ball has left your racket, it still remains lined up on your target. Before hitting, during the hit, after the hit - same aim. My father describes it this way:

"Keep the face of the racket squared on the intended line of flight as long as possible"

The reason that we do this is that you have very little chance of predicting exactly where you will make contact with the ball. Your opponent's shot is probably moving at 40 - 60 - 80 miles per hour. There's no way to guarantee that your racket will make contact with their ball at exactly the right moment that you are planning to hit it. It may be six inches farther forward than you planned, or three inches back, or even a foot forward or back. But if your racket face is aimed at the target during the entire shot, you give yourself a wide margin for error when you make contact with the ball.

People who swing at the volley miss this point (and the volley), because there is very little chance that they will time their stroke to correspond exactly with the flight of the ball at precisely the right moment to hit it where they want. The volley doesn't need your swing, since the incoming ball typically has tremendous pace. The friction of the air on the ball has had less time to slow it down, the slowing effect of the bounce on the ball hasn't happened - the ball hasn't bounced. The volley doesn't need much more power, just your quick, surgical punch, and it's the other guy's problem again.

One thing that seems to help people on the volley is to

V-2: involve the non-dominant hand.

What that means is that when you prepare for the shot take your non-hitting hand to the side that you are hitting on along with your hitting hand. This automatically turns your shoulder and gives your body the leverage to punch the ball effectively. By involving the non-dominant hand on every shot even though you aren't going to hit with it, you still create better racket preparation, which makes for successful volleying.

I like to practice the volley from the service line. That's called the "gateway to the net" by my father, the Ol' Coach. If you can get that volley, then you can get up to the net for the put-away volley. The put-away volley hardly needs practice. Even a bad volley at the net can be a winner, simply because you were there. It's the approach volley that gets you there. Spend equal time or more at the service line in your volley warm-up and practice.

The one thing to remember about the approach volley is to hit the ball higher over the net. You need to have a specific air target to hit through as you come in. One recent focus in tennis instruction has been the concept that the farther back you are in the court, the higher your ball should clear the airspace over the net in order to land in your opponent's backcourt. If you don't do this, your ball tends to land short and that is a clear invitation to the other player to come in and dominate the point at the net.

You should try to

V-3: penetrate an "air target"

of about two racket widths over the net on volleys hit from the service line. You need to hit the ball that high to make sure that you clear the net and get your volley deep in the court. Closer to the net you can have an air target of one racket width over the net.

The fascinating thing about this air target concept on volleys is that you may hit either up or down through the target.

If you are hitting a ball that arrives at your racket at a height that is above the air target, you are in luck. You are then hitting a mid to high volley and you can hit down through the air target (which is, again, an imaginary space that your ball passes through on its way over the net). If however, you are hitting a low volley, you have to hit it up through the same air target.

Most people seem to want to hit the ball three microns over the net, an extremely dramatic shot. The downsides to this shot are many. First of all, your dramatic shot has a fifty percent chance of being below your target, which means that in the race between the tortoise and the hare, you are the hare, i.e. - your volley went into the net and your date is going to start eyeing the conservative banker instead of you.

The other downside, not so obvious, is that if you are making contact with a volley that is below the net and you just barely clear the net, 90% of the time your shot will fall short in the court, and your opponent will get in to the net if they aren't already there and dominate the point.

By pretending that the net is one racket width higher on all close volleys, and two rackets higher on approach volleys, you will hit higher percentage, more effective, deeper volleys.

There are a lot of other things that you can work on to improve the volley: getting your knees bent, moving forward into the ball, hitting out in front, etc. Your pro will work with you on these things. The point is to practice them until they become automatic. Trust me, you want an automatic response when the ball is coming at you as hard as it does at the net. A short punching shot can be a great friend in such moments.

Chapter 12

Now What?

This book has introduced you to a method of incorporating individual tennis tips into real on-court situations. You can now use this tool to take what you learn in lessons, by reading tennis magazines or books, or from any source, and apply it to your game.

When you take a lesson, your pro may say many things to try to give you a picture of how to hit a stroke properly. Almost every one of your pro's statements is a candidate for a point project related to that stroke. If you practice the stroke with one point project at a time in mind, you eventually will assemble the whole stroke, and hopefully won't have to worry about the pieces anymore.

Good players are fascinated with the growth that they experience toward hitting better and better shots with more consistency and power. As you know, I like tinkering with my serve and seeing if I can squeeze out another few miles per hour by putting in more shoulder turn or more pronation.

I suggest that you review the list of point projects in the appendix of this book and then start your own list of things you want to work on. Your list may include items from my list, from things your pro has told you, or from experiences you've had in matches. And then you simply try them out.

You might write your active projects down on 3X5 note cards and bring them with you to your practice sessions or matches. You can look at the card between games in order to remind yourself of what you were hoping to work on today. This kind of purposeful practice turns your practice sessions, practice matches and actual competitive encounters into steps of progress in an ongoing process of planned development. This gives more meaning and direction to your tennis activities, and will take you to higher and higher skill levels and competitive success.

As your knowledge of tennis expands, I would encourage you to come up with your own ideas for point projects. Many pros might discourage this, but I feel that when someone puts attention on tennis, tennis slowly starts to reveal her secrets. I always feel like I have the right to invent something new, to come up with some new shot, some more efficient way to hit some stroke, etc. Since I have focused on tennis play and tennis teaching for many years it may come easier to me, but I think that simply observing what's going on on-court you really can eventually become your own (best) pro, and learn/invent things on your own.

You'll have to test those ideas in the laboratory of actual play situations. Some will turn out to be wrong, or hard to execute, or maybe funny looking, but some may actually do things that no one else has ever done. It's that kind of thinking that has allowed the expansion of tennis techniques over the years to the rich and still growing array of possible strokes that we now can choose from.

In any case, whether you discover new tennis techniques, or simply get more backhands over the net, using the point projects method puts you more in charge of your own tennis development, makes best use of the time and money you've put into learning the game, and makes you your own best tennis pro.

Appendix A

Match Record Plan

You might want to start keeping a notebook with a record of your matches in order to plan and schedule your point projects for further practice. The following points would be a good sample set of questions and answers to ask yourself:

Match record (Sample)

- Name of opponent
- Event
- Round (1st, 2nd, quarters, semis, final)
- Score
- Court surface
- Comments on successful areas
- Areas that need work

- How you won/lost points
- Conditioning elements
- Equipment performance
- Environmental factors
- Psychological factors
- Description of opponent's strengths and weaknesses
- Pre-visualization points
- Success of pre-visualization
- Tactical successes and potential growth areas
- Main principle learned by match
- Minor principles learned
- If you lost via the score, what was the overall win
- What would have to be different to win the match?
- Scouting report summary on this particular player
- Point projects for focus in future practices?

Appendix B

A basic list of point projects for the major strokes

Warm-Up Projects:

- Eyes on the ball all the way
- Shoulder turn first
- Hitting out in front
- Feet set for hit
- Bend the knees
- Low to high hit
- Get below the ball
- Valley up

Gap Projects

G-1: Reestablish your balance and optimal court position.
G-2: Watch the ball BEFORE your opponent hits it
G-3: Watch them hit the ball.
G-4: Split-step during their hit

G-5: Turn your shoulder first, and then move to the ball
G-6: Rise and fall with the ball,
G-7: Get the feet set by the time the ball bounces

Forehand

F-1: Set the racket when you "take it back"
F-2: Both arms go back
F-3: Get the racket face almost parallel to the ground on the backswing
F-4: Show them your back
F-5: Bisecting the path of the ball with your racket
F-6: "Valley up" through the ball
F-7: Bend your knees and get below every ball
F-8: Hit out in front

Backhand

B-1: Hitting out in front
B-2: Shorten up your backswing if you are rushed
B-3: Turn your shoulders first, and run with your shoulders turned
B-4: The non-dominant hand can support the racket
B-5: Set the head of the racket low on the backswing
B-6: Elbow bent
B-7: Get below the ball
B-8: Show them your back
B-9: Open a window shade

Serve

S-1: Show them your back

S-2: Bend the knees
S-3: Practice the toss
S-3: Toss on the side of your body
S-4: Watch the ball
S-5: Drop behind your back
S-6: Pronate
S-7: Hold the racket loosely
S-8: High backswing

Return of Serve

R-1: Watch that toss
R-2: Shoulder turn as soon as you detect which side the ball is going to
R-3: Get the racket below the ball
R-4: Hit the ball out in front
R-5: Split step during their toss
R-6: Watch the ball all the way to the racket
R-7: Full finish on the stroke
R-8: Have a target

Overhead

O-1: Racket up
O-2: Move
O-3: Set
O-4: Hit

Volley

V-1: Aim the shot for the entire shot
V-2: Involve the non-dominant hand
V-3: Penetrate an "air target"

Appendix C

How to find some real pros to help you achieve your own personal best

USPTA

See http://www.uspta.com and check out their "Find-A-Pro" service

USPTR

Call 1-800-421-6289

About the Author

Paul Stokstad is a creative and friendly type, with an extensive background in professional writing, teaching, and web marketing. He has a B.A. in English from the University of Iowa (1972) with a certificate for excellence in Creative Writing, and an M.A. from Iowa (1988) in English with an emphasis in Linguistics. He is also a certified USPTA tennis pro (P-1 rating).

He has been active in advertising copywriting and print publication management for 25 years, taught ad copywriting on the graduate level for ten years, and was an early adopter of web technologies, founding a web consulting and design group in 1996.

He has been playing and teaching tennis for over 40 years (no kidding, he was helping teach tennis clinics at age 12). His father was a successful teaching pro, and both brothers were state and regional tennis champions. He served as the Head Tennis Pro for the Burlington, Iowa Country Club for four years, and has also been active in the junior tennis clinic program in

Fairfield, Iowa for many years. He trained as a clinic pro at the Vic Braden Tennis College in Coto De Caza, California. He has taken USPTA continuing education courses in doubles tactics and System 5 and worked closely with the author of System 5 on clinic support documentation. He has served as an instructor in USPTA advanced junior development player camps, emphasizing the theme of this book.

He writes poetry, essays, ad copy, movie reviews, stand-up comedy, fiction, literary journalism, a humor column, a web marketing/design column, etc. He has many interests other than tennis, including improvisational theatre, Transcendental Meditation, poetry writing, and performance-oriented partner dance. He consults in web marketing and design, and has a website at http://www.stokstad.com and recently launched several peace-oriented websites:

http://www.peacecongress.us, and
http://www.peacestore.us.
http://www.peacecard.us

www.ingramcontent.com/pod-product-compliance
Lightning Source LLC
Chambersburg PA
CBHW021011090426
42738CB00007B/752